Blueprint for the Contingent Workforce

Strategies, Systems, and Success

by

Joel Schwan

I dedicate this book to:

My dad, Dr. Douglas Schwan, for his help with
revisions that saved me a lot of trouble.

And to:

My mom, Cheryl Lockard, and my wife, Kelly Schwan,
for being always supportive as I pursue my goals.

Table of Contents

Introduction

Welcome to the blueprint for the contingent workforce.

The Contingent Workforce Management (CWM) and Managed Service Provider (MSP) industry is experiencing substantial growth. The aftermath of the pandemic has amplified the demand for contingent workforce, driving this expansion. My name is Joel Schwan, and I've gained a lot of experience as a talent consultant. I've worked in IT Staffing with big clients like Uber, Microsoft, and Google, and I have also assisted in establishing and training program management offices as an enablement consultant with USAA and more.

This book is designed for talent consultants, program consultants, contingent workforce experts like me, and companies ready to explore the benefits of flexible labor arrangements. Here, we will journey through the essentials of contingent workforce management, combining my expert insights with a touch of humor for an engaging read—or at least, I'd hope it would be.

Let's start with a question: What exactly is the contingent workforce?

Well, if you're picturing a group of secret agents ready to parachute out of a plane at a moment's notice, you're not entirely wrong. The contingent workforce consists of individuals engaged in short-term contracts or project-based work. Unlike traditional employees, these workers offer their skills on a temporary basis, providing companies with a flexible way to manage projects and workload fluctuations. This book will guide you through managing this workforce effectively, from understanding the basics to implementing advanced strategies.

We'll proceed from an understanding of the basics to the implementation of advanced strategies.

The rise of contingent labor is nothing short of a revolution, changing the way businesses think about talent and how individuals view their careers. It's a tale of flexibility, innovation, and sometimes, just sheer necessity. But diving into this world without a guide would be like trying to kayak through white waters without a paddle. Exciting, but possibly catastrophic. That's where this introduction and the chapters that follow come in, paddle in hand, ready to navigate.

For those in the trenches - talent consultants, program consultants, and contingent workforce leaders - understanding the industry is paramount. Companies on the brink of adopting a contingent labor program will find that what lies ahead is not a one-size-fits-all strategy but a tailored suit that fits the unique contours of their business goals and culture. This book is tailored to help you craft that suit, stitch by meticulous stitch.

You might be wondering, "Is a contingent workforce strategy really for us?" or "How do we align our business goals with such a strategy?" These are valid questions and signal that you're ready to engage deeply with the material ahead. We'll explore designing effective program structures, aligning strategy with business goals, and much more. Consider this introduction your appetizer, whetting your appetite for the robust meal to come.

But it's not all strategy and no play. The contingent workforce world is also about navigating the intricate web of governance, understanding vendor neutrality, and selecting the right Vendor Management Systems (VMS). It's about differentiating between Managed Service Providers (MSP) and internal Program Management Offices (PMO), and it's about mastering the art of supplier management. Each chapter will peel back the layers of these topics, helping you to not only understand them but to use them to your advantage.

Now, let's talk about robots – yes, Artificial Intelligence (AI). AI is transforming the contingent workforce industry from talent acquisition to employee management. The role of AI in this industry is like that of a chess grandmaster, thinking several moves ahead and transforming strategy into victory. Our discussion will explore how leveraging AI can lead to improved decision making and efficiency.

Engagement strategies, metrics for success, and building a culture that supports contingent workers are also on the agenda. The balance of weaving contingent workers into the fabric of an organization's culture, creating an inclusive environment for all. This balance is as delicate as it is essential. Through humor, persuasive insights, and clear exposition, we'll tackle these topics head-on.

And, because we can't talk about the present without a nod to the future, we'll take a speculative leap into the technological innovations shaping the future of contingent workforce management. Preparing for what's next is not just about surviving; it's about thriving. It's about anticipating waves and being ready to surf them, rather than being caught off guard.

This exploration of the contingent workforce world will not follow a straight path. It will cover different ideas and methods, explore specific examples, and even branch off into the realm of legal and regulatory issues. Because this is an industry that is shaped by adaptability and innovation, it also requires careful and accurate guidance through the complicated legal terrain.

With each chapter, you'll find your grasp on the contingent workforce industry tightening, your understanding deepening, and your strategy taking shape. This book doesn't just aim to inform; it aims to transform. It endeavors to turn doubt into confidence, questions into strategies, and strategies into actions.

So, are you ready to start this journey? Are you ready to unlock the potential of the contingent workforce and transform the way your company views and engages talent? It's time to turn the page (figuratively speaking, of course) and dive into the fascinating world of contingent workforce management.

Remember, this isn't just about filling roles on a whim or responding to the latest trends. It's about building a strategic, responsive, and agile workforce that can adapt to changing business needs and propel your company into the future. Again, welcome to the world of the contingent workforce; your guide awaits.

Let's get started.

Chapter 1: Foundations of the Contingent Workforce

Think about exploring the complex world of the contingent workforce without a guide. It's like finding your way around a busy, unknown city without GPS. You might discover some interesting places, but you're likely to miss the hidden treasures and, to be fair, probably get a bit confused along the way. That's where this chapter comes in, providing both the direction and the landmarks to help talent consultants, contingent workforce leaders, and organizations interested in leveraging the potential of contingent labor navigate the industry. Our exploration is not just about learning what makes the contingent workforce work but also understanding the subtleties and nuances that shape it.

It's important to first break down the different types of contingent workers to understand how each contributes to an organization's success. By segmenting this workforce, we can optimize strategies for talent acquisition and performance management. The contingent workforce, broadly defined, is a labor pool consisting of individuals engaged by organizations on a non-permanent basis. This includes freelancers, independent contractors, consultants, and those employed through staffing agencies. While it's tempting to lump all non-permanent roles into one category, the reality is far more nuanced. Independent contractors, for example, bring specific expertise and autonomy, often hired directly by organizations for short-term projects or consultancy roles. Freelancers provide on-demand services, frequently in creative or technical sectors, offering flexibility for organizations that need specialized skills for one-off projects. Temporary agency workers help fill short-term gaps during peak workloads, and unlike freelancers or independent contractors, they are usually employed by a third-party staffing agency. Each of these contingent workers requires unique management strategies to ensure maximum efficiency and productivity. By recognizing these categories, businesses can better tailor their contingent workforce strategies, ensuring they leverage the right talent for the right tasks at the right time. The surge in contingent labor is driven by multiple factors. Technological advancements, such as digital platforms (e.g., Upwork, Fiverr, and TaskRabbit), have expanded access to global talent and enabled remote work, dissolving traditional geographical limitations. Economic shifts, particularly in response to financial downturns like the 2008 recession and the COVID-19 pandemic, have pushed organizations to adopt more flexible staffing models. These trends allow businesses to scale up or down efficiently without the long-term costs of permanent hires, making contingent labor an attractive option. These drivers demand a deeper look, not just a skim off the top, to truly grasp how they mold the fabric of contingent work.

Before sprinting ahead to strategize and optimize, it's crucial to establish a solid foundation. Understanding the contingent workforce industry involves deciphering the blend of flexibility and structure that these workers bring to the table. It's about recognizing the dual need for agility in responding to business needs and the rigor required to manage this unique workforce effectively. The following sections will zoom in on the rise of contingent labor and untangle the terminologies and definitions that often act as stumbling blocks. With each turn of the page, the aim is to transition from seeing the contingent workforce as a mere alternative to appreciating it as a strategic component of modern business. So, let's ease into this journey with a mix of curiosity and enthusiasm, ready to be enlightened on crafting a contingent labor program that stands not just on the brink of innovation but also on the right side of it.

Understanding the Contingent Workforce Industry

Entering the realm of contingent labor feels a bit like stepping into a parallel universe where traditional employment norms are turned on their head. Here, flexibility is king, and the workforce resembles more of a chameleon, adeptly changing colors to match corporate needs. It's a bustling marketplace, a carnival of talent, with jugglers, acrobats, and magicians (or developers, designers, and project managers, in less metaphorical terms) ready to showcase their skills on demand.

But let's strip away the carnival analogy for a moment. At its core, the contingent workforce industry is about connecting businesses with non-permanent labor - thinkers and doers who aren't tethered to a single employer but instead, flit from project to project, bringing fresh perspectives and specialized skills. It's a model that's been gaining tremendous momentum, propelled by the twin engines of technological advancement and a generational shift towards valuing flexibility and work-life balance. However, for those tasked with navigating this industry—whether you're a talent consultant, a contingent workforce leader, or a company looking to dip your toes in these waters—there are nuances and complexities aplenty.

First off, understanding the contingent workforce industry requires recognizing its kaleidoscope of participants. From traditional freelancers to workers engaged through staffing agencies, from independent contractors to professionals tapped via Managed Service Providers (MSPs) and gig platforms, the definitions are as varied as the workers themselves. Each brings its own set of expectations, working styles, and, yes, even complications. Navigating this requires not just a strong grasp of the different types of contingent labor but also an understanding of the legal and operational quicksand you might encounter.

Operationalizing a contingent workforce strategy requires meticulous planning and an understanding of both legal and operational challenges. From navigating worker classifications to ensuring compliance with labor laws across different regions, each decision must be made with precision. Organizations that master this balance can create a dynamic, resilient workforce, but failing to address these complexities can result in significant legal and financial repercussions. The picture only comes together seamlessly when each piece is carefully and thoughtfully placed. This involves not just understanding who your contingent workers are but also how to engage, manage, and retain them effectively within the legal frameworks of your region and industry. It's a strategic dance that, when done right, can lead to unparalleled agility and innovation within organizations.

So, as we venture deeper into this conversation, remember that the contingent workforce industry, with all its moving parts and players, is not just about filling temporary positions. It's about constructing a resilient, adaptive organization that thrives on the very principles of dynamism and flexibility. It's challenging, sure, but for those willing to embrace the adventure, the rewards can be as thrilling as a high-wire act—minus the safety net.

The Rise of Contingent Labor

In the complex and interrelated fabric of today's work environment, a remarkable change is happening, indicating a move away from conventional work models to more adaptable and agile ones. This is the time of contingent labor, a field full of possibilities, creativity, and yes, some challenging intricacies..

For starters, let's demystify what we mean by contingent labor. Essentially, it encapsulates those jet-setters of the work world who orbit around projects and roles—not tethered by the conventional bonds of permanent employment. They're the freelancers, contractors, consultants, and sometimes, the unsung heroes filling in temporary roles with gusto and a suitcase full of skills.

Why the surge, you might ask? Ah, an excellent question that unravels the fabric of economic, technological, and societal shifts. One can't ignore the siren song of flexibility that contingent work sings both to employers and talent. For organizations, the allure lies in the agility to scale workforce up or down, adapting swiftly to market demands without the overheads of traditional hiring. Talent, on the flip side, relishes the autonomy, varied exposure, and in many cases, the work-life balance that contingent roles offer. It's a match made in heaven, albeit one requiring meticulous orchestration.

The technological revolution—a co-conspirator in this narrative—deserves a spotlight. With digital platforms enabling remote work, the geographical barriers that once constrained talent pools have dissolved like sugar in tea. Suddenly, a developer in Bangalore can contribute to a project in Silicon Valley, while wearing pajamas, no less! This global talent marketplace, facilitated by innovative tools and platforms, has not just expanded access but has also intensified the competition and diversity in the contingent labor pool.

Economically speaking, let's not overlook the impact of financial downturns. In the shadow of recessions, companies tend to tighten belts, making the flexibility of contingent labor even more appealing. It's a survival strategy, allowing businesses to remain nimble, innovate, and perhaps most crucially, persist through economic ebbs and flows without the commitment of permanent hires.

However, it's not all sunshine and rainbows. With the rise of contingent labor comes the challenge of integration. How do you ensure these flexible workers mesh well with your permanent teams? How do you maintain culture, continuity, and quality? Ah, the plot thickens, and the need for strategic workforce planning and management becomes ever so pronounced.

There's also the legislative labyrinth to navigate. With different countries and states applying varied lenses to contingent work classifications, legal compliance becomes a tightrope walk. It's intricate, it's baffling, and yes, getting it wrong can be costly. Navigating this requires a blend of legal acumen and strategic foresight—a cocktail not everyone can mix well.

The data dance is another fascinating aspect of this evolution. In the age of information, understanding the dynamics of your contingent workforce through robust data analytics is not just an advantage; it's a necessity. This intelligence empowers organizations to make informed decisions, optimize workforce mix, and anticipate future needs with a degree of precision previously unattainable.

Moreover, the cultural shift towards valuing diversity and experiences over traditional career trajectories is fueling the contingent labor flame. The narrative of a successful career is being rewritten, no longer confined to the ladder-climbing pursuits within the walls of a single organization. The burgeoning gig economy champions a portfolio of varied experiences, fostering a more dynamic and adaptable workforce.

Vendor Management Systems (VMS) and Managed Service Providers (MSP) play crucial roles in orchestrating contingent labor. These tools provide the necessary infrastructure to manage vendor relationships, ensure compliance, and track worker performance, all while giving organizations visibility into their contingent workforce. MSPs, in particular, offer expert guidance in navigating complex labor laws and regulations, ensuring that organizations can scale their contingent workforce efficiently and legally. These entities and tools serve as the orchestrators, ensuring that the symphony of contingent labor doesn't descend into cacophony. They provide the structure, processes, and oversight necessary to manage this complex ecosystem effectively.

Indeed, the rise of contingent labor intersects with the broader trends of workplace flexibility, digital transformation, and the pursuit of work-life harmony. It encapsulates the desire for work that adapts to life, not the other way around—a desire that seems increasingly achievable in today's interconnected, digital-first world.

Yet, embracing contingent labor is not a panacea without its pitfalls. The challenges of cohesion, culture, compliance, and control lurk beneath the surface, waiting to test the mettle of organizations bold enough to navigate this terrain. It requires a new playbook—one that values adaptability, strategic planning, and an inclusive approach to workforce management.

As we stand at this crossroads, looking toward an uncertain yet invigorating horizon, the rise of contingent labor presents both a promise and a puzzle. Organizations that master this balance, leveraging the strengths while mitigating the risks, will not just survive; they'll thrive, crafting a workforce as dynamic and resilient as the world around them.

The wave of contingent labor is upon us, reshaping the bedrock of employment and workforce management. It beckons with opportunities for innovation, flexibility, and strategic advantage, yet it demands vigilance, strategy, and an empathetic understanding of the human element within this paradigm. For talent consultants, contingent workforce leaders, and organizations poised at the edge of this transformation, the journey ahead is as daunting as it is exhilarating. The era of contingent labor is here, redefining the essence of work, one gig at a time.

Deciphering Contingent Workforce Dictionary Dilemmas (Terminologies and Definitions)

We've all been there, staring blank-eyed at a jargon-packed document, wondering if it's in English, Spanish, or Klingon (you cannot truly appreciate contingent workforce jargon until you've heard it in the original Klingon). Particularly, the contingent workforce industry loves its acronyms and esoteric terms. They're tossed around like confetti at a New Year's Eve party, leaving the uninitiated scratching their heads. Fear not! This chapter is your Rosetta Stone, the key to unlocking these mysteries without needing a decoder ring.

First off, let's tackle a biggie: MSP and VMS. These aren't new bands on the Billboard charts. An MSP, or **Managed Service Provider**, is akin to the conductor of an orchestra, ensuring all parts of your contingent workforce program are playing in harmony. It is an external organization engaged to manage an organization's contingent workforce program. MSPs are responsible for the end-to-end management of temporary staffing vendors, including selection, performance monitoring, compliance, and reporting.

Meanwhile, a VMS, or **Vendor Management System**, is the digital backbone, the technology that helps manage and streamline the process. Think of the MSP as the why and the how, and the VMS as the what and the where. The process we are talking about is the procurement and management of the temporary and contingent labor, including requisition, sourcing, assessment, hiring, management, and payment of temporary workers. Then there's the term 'contingent workforce' itself. It might sound like a group of mercenaries from a sci-fi novel, but it's just industry-speak for non-permanent labor, including freelancers, contractors, and temporary workers. They're the utility players of the working world, versatile and ready at a moment's notice.

But wait, there's more...

Agile Workforce: Refers to a workforce that is highly adaptable and flexible, capable of quickly responding to changing business needs and project demands.

Bill Rate vs. Pay Rate: The bill rate is the amount a client pays to a staffing agency for the services of a contingent worker. The pay rate is the amount that the worker receives. The difference between these rates constitutes the staffing agency's margin.

Competitive Bid: A procurement scenario where multiple suppliers are invited to submit bids for a project or Statement of Work (SOW), promoting competition and potentially leading to better value for the client.

Compliance Management: The process of ensuring that all contingent workforce engagements comply with relevant laws, regulations, and organizational policies, thereby mitigating legal and financial risks.

Consultants: Project-based labor workers who are usually acquired through a Statement of Work (SOW) contract. They possess expertise in specific fields and are typically managed by the consulting firm engaged by the organization.

Contingent Staffing: The provision of workers by suppliers to organizations on a non-permanent basis, including temporary workers, contractors, and consultants.

Co-employment Risk: The legal and tax implications that arise when an employee is shared between two entities, such as a staffing agency and the end-client. Proper management of co-employment risk is essential to avoid legal complications.

Deliverable/Milestone: Terms used to describe the outputs or outcomes of a project. Deliverables are the specific work products or services to be provided, while milestones mark significant points or stages in a project's progress.

Direct Sourcing: A strategy where organizations recruit contingent workers directly, bypassing traditional staffing agencies. This can lead to cost savings and greater engagement with the contingent workforce.

Engagement Strategies: Approaches for effectively integrating and managing contingent workers within an organization, ensuring they are motivated, productive, and aligned with the company's goals.

Enterprise Resource Planning (ERP): Software systems that integrate all facets of an operation, including planning, purchasing, inventory, sales, marketing, finance, human resources, and more.

Fixed Bid: A pricing structure where a single price is agreed upon for the entire scope of work or project, regardless of the actual time and materials used.

Gig Worker: Individuals who undertake short-term, flexible jobs, often facilitated by digital platforms. This term is synonymous with the gig economy, where temporary positions are common, and organizations contract with independent workers for short-term engagements.

Human Resource Information System (HRIS): A software or online solution that assists in managing employee data and human resource policies and procedures. It often includes functionalities for payroll, benefits administration, time and attendance, and more.

Independent Contractor: A type of worker who operates under a business-to-business contract, providing services to a client under terms specified in a contract or agreement.

IR35: Tax legislation designed to combat tax avoidance by workers, and the firms hiring them, who work as employees in all but name through an intermediary, such as a limited company, but do not pay the corresponding income tax and national insurance contributions.

Program Management: The process of managing multiple related projects with the intention of improving an organization's performance. In the context of contingent workforce management, it involves overseeing the various aspects of the program to ensure efficiency and effectiveness.

Recruitment Process Outsourcing (RPO): A form of business process outsourcing where an employer transfers all or part of its recruitment processes to an external service provider.

Resource Tracking: A process or system used to monitor and manage the deployment and utilization of temporary and contract workers across an organization. It helps ensure compliance, optimize resource allocation, and maintain security.

Services Procurement: The acquisition of services in a way that optimizes cost, quality, and service delivery. It involves strategic sourcing, vendor management, and contract management for services rather than goods.

SOW (Statement of Work): A document that captures and defines all aspects of a project, including activities, deliverables, timelines, and payment terms. It forms the basis of the agreement between the client and the service provider for project-based work.

Staffing Agencies: Organizations that provide temporary workers, contractors, or permanent placements to businesses. They handle recruitment, screening, and payroll for the workers they place.

Supplier Management: The process of managing relationships with vendors that supply goods and services to an organization, ensuring they meet the company's standards for cost, quality, and delivery.

Talent Pool: A database or list of potential candidates that an organization can draw upon to fill vacant positions, especially for contingent or temporary roles.

Temporary Labor: Workers hired for a specific, limited period, often through staffing agencies. This includes seasonal workers, project-based workers, and others hired for a short duration.

Total Talent Management: A holistic approach to managing all human resources, including permanent employees and contingent workers, to achieve a comprehensive understanding and optimization of workforce capabilities.

Vendor on Premises (VOP): A situation where a representative of a staffing agency works on-site at the client's location to manage the temporary workforce more effectively, providing a direct liaison between the staffing agency and the client.

While the contingent workforce's vernacular can be bewildering, it's also the key to unlocking its potential. With this chapter as your guide, you're well on your way to becoming a contingent workforce linguist, adept at translating its complexities into strategies for success. Remember, every term you master is a step towards leveraging the full power of the contingent workforce, transforming what once seemed like inscrutable Kling—err, jargon into a strategic advantage for your organization.

Chapter 2: Contingent Workforce Program Strategy

After laying down the foundational bricks about the contingent workforce, it's time to dive into the riveting world of strategy, where creativity meets logic. Picture yourself as a maestro, orchestrating an eclectic mix of talent, where every note must harmonize with your business's symphony. Crafting a Contingent Workforce Program Strategy isn't just about filling positions; it's about aligning a dynamic and flexible talent pool with the pulsating beat of your business goals. Now, imagine doing that without missing a beat. Thrilling, isn't it?

Creating a good program structure is like preparing a stage for a great show. Each role, from lighting to sound, is important, and in the business context, it means knowing the clear and flexible roles of your contingent talent. The strategy must be flexible, adjustable, and responsive to market changes, similar to improvisation in a jazz performance. But there's a twist - this improvisation is intentional, based on solid knowledge and strategic vision.

Aligning your contingent workforce strategy with overarching business goals is essential for driving organizational success. It's not just about sourcing top talent—it's about strategically positioning that talent to meet specific, measurable business objectives. This requires a clear understanding of current operational challenges, as well as the future capabilities needed to propel the business forward. By identifying key performance indicators (KPIs) related to cost savings, time-to-fill roles, or innovation, organizations can ensure that their contingent workforce is a driver of business growth rather than merely a stop-gap solution. Think of it as being a visionary architect; you wouldn't add a state-of-the-art kitchen to an ancient castle, would you? Instead, you'd find a way to blend innovation with tradition, ensuring every addition enhances the whole.

While discussing strategies, it's also important to highlight the importance of having a diverse toolkit. In today's fast-paced world, sticking to a single strategy is akin to trying to play a symphony with just a flute. Sure, a flute is beautiful, but it can't capture the depth and richness a full orchestra can. Therefore, your approach should be multifaceted, incorporating elements like technology, analytics, and human intuition.

Crafting a Contingent Workforce Program Strategy is an art and science, demanding creativity, precision, and a dash of daring. It's about setting the stage for innovation, aligning with your business's cadence, and conducting a performance that resonates with success. As you turn the page, remember, the strategies you lay down today are the stepping stones for the milestones you aspire to achieve tomorrow. Let's make each step count.

Designing an Effective Program Structure

Designing a contingent workforce program structure that is both resilient and successful requires adaptability, but it also demands clear guidelines. Just as an architect drafts blueprints before construction, your program should have well-defined roles and responsibilities for every stakeholder involved, including HR, procurement, and hiring managers. Flexibility must be carefully balanced with control; while the program should remain responsive to market fluctuations and evolving talent demands, strong governance is essential to ensure compliance and consistent performance. A successful program structure, much like a well-built foundation, must be both strong and adaptable, ensuring that it supports the organization's strategic objectives while allowing for the integration of new workforce solutions.

Your program structure is the foundation of your contingent workforce management, like a stage that can hold a large and diverse performance. And just as a solid stage can enable a successful show, a well-planned program structure can meet an organization's varied needs, becoming the key to your contingent workforce strategy.

Before we go any further, let's acknowledge the obvious: there's no single solution here. Each organization has its own needs, goals, and existing processes that are different from anyone else's. Therefore, the first step to finding an effective program is to thoroughly understand your organization's pulse – its main needs, objectives, and the problems faced by its contingent workforce.

Building on that, the foundation of an effective program structure is flexibility coupled with robustness. Imagine designing a building in an area prone to earthquakes. You wouldn't just focus on making it strong; you'd make it flexible enough to withstand shocks. Similarly, a contingent workforce program must be designed to quickly adapt to market changes, talent availability, and technological advancements, all while maintaining operational stability.

At the heart of a thriving program are clear communication channels. In a symphony, if the violins are out of sync with the cellos, it disrupts the harmony. Similarly, ensuring that all stakeholders – from hiring managers to vendors, from procurement to HR – have a shared understanding and aligned goals, is key to avoiding discord.

Technology has an important role in the success of contingent workforce programs. Leveraging a Vendor Management System (VMS) is akin to reinforcing a structure with cutting-edge tools that enhance its durability. VMS automates key processes, from requisition management to candidate selection, while providing real-time visibility into program performance. In addition, the integration of AI-driven solutions enables more precise forecasting, skill matching, and risk management, allowing organizations to make informed, data-driven decisions at every stage of the workforce lifecycle. This ensures operational efficiency and supports long-term business goals.. And just like how every building needs a different approach to seismic reinforcement, the selection and implementation of technology will vary based on your program's unique requirements and scale.

Another cornerstone is governance. A robust governance structure ensures that the program remains compliant with laws and regulations, mitigates risks, and adheres to best practices. It's akin to building codes and inspections ensuring that our metaphorical building is safe and compliant.

Selecting the right engagement models is critical for optimizing both cost and outcomes. For project-based work with clearly defined deliverables, a Statement of Work (SOW) engagement model may offer the most control and accountability. Freelancers or gig workers are ideal for tasks that require niche expertise or a quick turnaround, offering flexibility at a lower cost. Temporary workers sourced through staffing agencies are best suited for filling short-term labor needs or covering seasonal peaks. When deciding which model to use, consider the complexity of the task, duration, and the level of oversight required. Whether it's Statement of Work (SOW), independent contractors, or temporary staff through staffing agencies, the selection needs to align with the work's nature and desired outcomes.

Supplier management is not just about maintaining relationships—it's about ensuring that suppliers consistently deliver on their promises. Organizations should implement formalized supplier performance scorecards to track critical metrics, such as quality of hire, response times, and compliance with labor regulations. Regular evaluations and feedback loops foster continuous improvement and ensure that suppliers remain aligned with your strategic goals. Additionally, clear and detailed contracts should outline expectations, performance metrics, and penalties for non-compliance, helping mitigate risks and secure high-quality outcomes. To achieve this, organizations must establish clear performance metrics, including response time, quality of hires, and compliance with contractual terms. Regular evaluation of suppliers through a formalized process, such as scorecards and reviews, helps maintain high standards and fosters continuous improvement in talent delivery.

Metrics and KPIs are the compass that guides your program, allowing you to measure performance, track progress, and make necessary adjustments. Key KPIs might include time-to-fill roles, cost savings per hire, and contractor retention rates. Additionally, tracking worker satisfaction, compliance rates, and spend under management will offer deeper insights into both the effectiveness of your engagement strategy and the overall health of your workforce program. Regular reviews of these metrics allow for iterative improvements, ensuring the program remains aligned with business objectives. And remember, in the dynamic world of contingent workforce management, regular review, and adjustment of these metrics is key.

Now, let's talk innovation. Innovation is the driving force behind successful contingent workforce programs. Artificial Intelligence (AI) tools can now streamline talent matching by analyzing candidate profiles and predicting the best fit for open roles, significantly reducing time-to-hire. Blockchain technology is increasingly used for smart contracts, ensuring secure, automated contract execution and reducing administrative burdens. Data analytics platforms allow organizations to forecast workforce needs, manage costs, and monitor compliance in real time, while robotic process automation (RPA) can automate routine tasks like onboarding and payroll. By leveraging these technologies, companies can not only improve efficiency but also enhance their decision-making processes.

Integration into the broader HR and procurement strategies is also vital. Your contingent workforce program shouldn't be an island but a seamless part of your organization's talent management and procurement teams. This integration ensures alignment of goals and streamlines processes across departments.

Lastly, never underestimate the power of culture. Just as a building is more than its walls and beams, a contingent workforce program is more than its processes and technologies. Fostering a culture of inclusion for contingent workers is not just beneficial for morale—it can significantly improve engagement and performance. Consider hosting onboarding sessions tailored to contingent staff, helping them understand company values and expectations. Encouraging participation in team-building activities and company-wide meetings can also make contingent workers feel more connected to the organization. Additionally, implementing performance reviews for contingent staff allows them to receive feedback and feel valued, which can enhance retention and productivity. By creating an inclusive culture, you not only integrate contingent workers effectively but also elevate your program's overall success.

Designing an effective contingent workforce program structure is akin to orchestrating a masterpiece. It requires a balance of strength and flexibility, a deep understanding of your unique industry, and the harmonious integration of various elements. And while the process can be complex, the outcome - a resilient, responsive, and strategic contingent workforce program - is well worth the effort.

So, as you embark on this exciting journey, remember, it's all about crafting a structure that not just exists but excels, in tune with the evolving dynamics of the contingent workforce. Let's turn what might seem like a daunting task into an opportunity to innovate, lead, and achieve strategic success.

Aligning Strategy with Business Goals

When you manage a contingent workforce, you need to match your strategy with your business goals. This is not just a good idea; it's essential for long-term success. Running a contingent workforce program without a clear connection to your business objectives is like navigating a ship without a map. Every decision, from staffing to project execution, must be aligned with overarching business goals to ensure that contingent talent contributes meaningfully to organizational success. Defining this alignment from the start not only provides direction but also ensures that resources are deployed efficiently, driving both short-term and long-term results. Let's get rid of that fog and ensure every action is intentional and effective.

To start with, understanding the overarching business objectives is crucial. Whether it's increasing agility, driving innovation, or cutting costs, your contingent workforce program should directly contribute to these goals. It's like matching the pieces of a puzzle - it may seem challenging at first, but with the right perspective, the pieces fit perfectly, revealing a bigger picture that benefits the entire organization.

Let's be honest, the rapid evolution of the modern workforce requires businesses to stay agile, and the contingent workforce offers the flexibility to adapt swiftly. It serves as a versatile talent pool that organizations can leverage to fill skills gaps, address short-term demands, and respond to dynamic market conditions. The key lies in ensuring that your contingent workforce strategy is integrated with your broader business goals, allowing for scalable solutions that meet both immediate and long-term needs.. By aligning your strategy with business goals, you're not just filling gaps; you're anticipating future needs and positioning your organization as a formidable competitor in your industry.

Setting clear, measurable goals is essential for aligning your contingent workforce strategy with business objectives. For example, you might track **time-to-fill positions**, **project completion rates**, or **cost savings per engagement** to evaluate the effectiveness of your workforce program. By establishing KPIs that reflect your organization's strategic priorities, you can ensure that every contingent worker contributes to business growth and operational efficiency. If your business objective is to improve project turnaround times, quantify what success looks like. Is it a 20% improvement? A reduction in specific project phases? By defining these metrics, you can better structure your contingent workforce to meet these targets.

Collaboration across departments is also essential. Your contingent workforce strategy shouldn't operate in a silo. Engage with stakeholders from finance, HR, and operations to ensure alignment and support. It's like conducting an orchestra, where every section needs to be in tune for a flawless performance.

Risks and challenges are part of the journey. Identifying potential roadblocks, such as compliance issues or skill shortages, and developing contingency plans, ensures that your strategy is realistic and resilient. Think of these challenges as the plot twists in a best-selling novel - they keep things interesting and test your strategy's solidity.

Embracing technology is no longer optional; it's essential. Leveraging a Vendor Management System (VMS) or Artificial Intelligence (AI) can streamline processes, provide valuable insights, and enhance decision-making. It's like upgrading from a manual transmission to an automatic; the right tools can make the journey smoother and more efficient.

Remember, communication is king. Regular updates, feedback loops, and open channels of communication keep everyone on the same page and foster a culture of transparency and trust. This isn't just about sending out emails; it's about creating a dialogue where ideas and concerns can be shared freely.

Training and development play a pivotal role. A strategy that includes upskilling and reskilling your contingent workforce not only aligns with business goals of innovation and growth but also builds a more engaged and productive talent pool. Think of it as investing in the seeds of a garden, nurturing growth that will eventually bloom into success.

Finally, don't forget about the human element. A strategy that aligns with business goals should also consider the needs and aspirations of the contingent workers. After all, they're not just resources; they're individuals with unique skills and perspectives that can enrich your organization. Creating an inclusive environment that recognizes their contributions is like watering that garden we mentioned - it encourages growth and sustainability.

Aligning your contingent workforce strategy with business goals is not just a one-time task; it's an ongoing process of adaptation and refinement. It's about being proactive, staying agile, and always keeping the end goal in sight. By taking these steps, you're not just ensuring that your contingent workforce program is effective; you're turning it into a strategic powerhouse that drives your business forward.

So, let's move beyond the fog and navigate towards a future where your contingent workforce strategy and business goals are so seamlessly aligned that success becomes not just a possibility, but a certainty. The road ahead is clear, and with the right approach, there's nothing stopping you from achieving greatness. Together, let's turn those business goals into milestones of success, one strategic step at a time.

Building a Case for Procurement Services

Organizations are increasing their reliance on an extended workforce, encompassing temp labor, contractors, freelancers, and outsourced workers. This diversity allows companies to remain agile, quickly adapting to market changes and minimizing fixed costs. However, the inclusion of non-employee labor is not without its challenges, introducing significant risks and complexities into workforce management. Services procurement emerges as a strategic solution, aiming to actively manage all categories of non-employee labor while ensuring compliance with laws and regulations, thereby safeguarding the organization.

Services procurement is no longer just an operational necessity; it is a strategic lever that can drive significant business advantages. At its core, it enables organizations to manage contractors and contingent staff with precision, ensuring not only compliance with legal requirements but also optimization in terms of cost, performance, and workforce flexibility. By taking a proactive approach to services procurement, organizations can mitigate risks, reduce operational costs, and improve access to specialized talent, all while maintaining a high level of service quality. The adoption of a robust services procurement program is crucial for organizations seeking not only to mitigate risks associated with non-employee labor but also to harness the full potential of a flexible workforce. This section elucidates the critical importance of services procurement in modern workforce management.

To advocate for the integration of services procurement into organizational practices, a well-structured business case is essential. This part of the eBook provides a detailed, step-by-step guide to crafting a compelling argument in favor of adopting services procurement strategies. Key considerations outlined include:

- **Questions to Ask:** Begin by understanding the specific needs of your organization and the scope of non-employee labor utilized. Identifying what information is necessary and where to source it lays the groundwork for a persuasive business case.

- **Risk Assessment:** Conducting a thorough risk assessment is critical for a successful services procurement strategy. This involves identifying the risks associated with non-employee labor, such as misclassification, co-employment risks, or contract breaches, and developing mitigation strategies to address these issues proactively. A well-structured risk assessment should also weigh these risks against potential rewards, including cost savings, access to specialized skills, and workforce flexibility, while clearly outlining the expected return on investment (ROI). Developing contingency plans for key risk areas can ensure that your organization remains resilient in the face of challenges. This analysis demonstrates the strategic value of services procurement in mitigating risks while maximizing benefits.

- **Organizing Elements:** Successful business cases are well-organized and compelling. This section highlights how to arrange all necessary components, from risk assessments to benefits, in a manner that garners executive approval.

Services procurement offers a myriad of benefits that extend beyond mere compliance and risk mitigation:

- **Confident Procurement:** Secure access to professional and support service resources at competitive prices, ensuring that your organization can leverage the best talent and services available.

- **Resource Tracking:** Implement systems that seamlessly track all non-employees, including those not engaged through centralized sourcing, providing a comprehensive view of the extended workforce.

- **Direct Sourcing & Talent Pools:** Direct sourcing allows organizations to tap into top-tier talent by leveraging their brand equity, eliminating the need for third-party staffing agencies. Building talent pools—databases of

vetted candidates who can be mobilized quickly—
provides significant workforce agility. These pools allow
organizations to respond to urgent project needs or skill
shortages more efficiently, reducing both time-to-hire
and overall costs. Furthermore, by maintaining an
engaged talent pool, organizations can foster long-term
relationships with contingent workers, ensuring a
consistent pipeline of skilled talent. By establishing and
maintaining talent pools, companies can quickly mobilize
skilled individuals as needs arise.

Integrating services procurement into your workforce
management strategy is not just a tactical move—it's a strategic
imperative that significantly enhances organizational agility and
competitive advantage. In an era where the flexibility of the
workforce is directly linked to operational success, services
procurement stands as a pillar of modern business strategy. Now
is the opportune moment to embrace services procurement,
positioning your organization to thrive in the dynamic business
landscape of tomorrow.

Chapter 3: Contingent Workforce Program Governance

Entering Contingent Workforce Program Governance marks a critcal juncture where strategic oversight and operational discipline meet. Governance is not just an operational checkpoint; it is the framework that ensures your contingent workforce program thrives under the pressures of legal, ethical, and performance standards. The cornerstone of any contingent workforce program isn't its ability to dazzle with jargon (though, admittedly, that has its place), but robust governance that ensures the program not only survives but thrives.

Governance, in the context of contingent workforce programs, is akin to having a world-class conductor at the helm of an orchestra; every note hits just right, and harmony prevails even in the face of a potentially discordant ensemble. This chapter delves into the principles and practices that form the backbone of effective governance. We'll explore setting standards, ensuring compliance, and the pivotal role leadership plays in steering the ship. The goal? To ensure our contingent workforce program is as fine-tuned and well-oiled as a luxury Swiss watch.

The first port of call in our governance journey is establishing clear standards. It's not enough to simply have rules; these rules need to be the guiding North Star for all program stakeholders. Compliance is not just a regulatory requirement; it is the bedrock of your program's credibility. Without a strong focus on compliance, the entire structure of your workforce management could face severe legal, financial, and operational risks.

Implementing a robust compliance framework ensures that your contingent workforce program adheres to local, national, and international laws, protecting your organization from costly errors. Without a steadfast commitment to compliance, we're essentially building our castle on sand - not the most strategic of choices.

However, the true linchpin in our governance framework is leadership. Think of it as the secret sauce that brings everything together. Leaders are not merely enforcers of rules; they are the architects of a governance culture that resonates throughout the organization. To foster an environment where governance principles are embraced, leadership must take proactive steps:

1. **Set the Tone from the Top:**
   Leadership must consistently demonstrate a commitment to governance by aligning their actions with organizational policies. This visible adherence to governance standards, whether through personal conduct, decision-making, or day-to-day interactions, sets a strong example for the entire workforce, contingent and permanent alike.

2. **Engage in Transparent Communication:**
   Regular, transparent communication from leadership is key to fostering trust and ensuring that governance policies are understood and respected. Leaders should frequently communicate the 'why' behind governance policies, ensuring that all team members, including contingent workers, see the bigger picture and understand how compliance contributes to organizational success.

3. **Provide Resources for Compliance:**
   Effective governance cannot exist in a vacuum. Leaders

must ensure that the necessary resources—whether tools, training, or personnel—are available to facilitate compliance. This includes implementing systems such as Vendor Management Systems (VMS) to track contingent workers' activities and providing continuous learning opportunities related to governance best practices.

4. **Encourage Accountability Across All Levels:**
   Leadership should promote a culture of accountability by implementing clear role-based expectations and consequences. By embedding accountability into performance reviews and governance audits, leaders create a structured environment where everyone understands their role in maintaining compliance, from executives to contingent workers.

5. **Facilitate Continuous Improvement:**
   Governance is not static; it evolves with the business and regulatory environment. Leaders must commit to continuous improvement by regularly reviewing governance policies, seeking feedback from stakeholders, and making necessary adjustments. This forward-thinking approach ensures that governance frameworks remain relevant and effective in the face of change.

By fostering transparency, promoting ethical standards, and driving a commitment to compliance, leaders can ensure that governance is not just adhered to, but actively embraced as a core value across all levels of the organization. Regular training, communication, and visible adherence to governance principles by leadership are critical to building this culture. It's about leading by example and cultivating a culture where everyone understands the 'why' behind the 'what'. This is where the magic happens, transcending mere compliance to genuinely embed governance into the fabric of the program.

In summary, governance in the contingent workforce sector isn't a tick-box exercise; it's the very essence that determines whether a program simply exists or excels. From setting the stage with clear standards to ensuring each note of compliance is played to perfection, and ultimately harmonizing it all with inspired leadership - governance is the symphony that leads to success. So, let's fine-tune our instruments and get ready for a performance that's nothing short of spectacular.

Principles and Practices for Robust Governance

As we pivot from understanding the foundational aspects of the contingent workforce to examining the gears and cogs that keep the system well-oiled, we stumble upon the cornerstone of any successful contingent labor program: robust governance. It's an area often overlooked, yet as crucial as the morning coffee that jump-starts our day. In this chapter, we'll dive into the principles and practices that not only prop up but also propel forward a contingent workforce program that is both efficient and resilient.

The first principle is straightforward yet profound: clarity is king. When it comes to governance, ambiguity is the archenemy. Establishing crystal clear guidelines, roles, responsibilities, and processes is akin to providing a roadmap in an unfamiliar city. It ensures that everyone involved, from the leader to the last contractor, knows exactly where they're going and how to get there. But let's remember, clarity without flexibility is like a rigid old tree that snaps in the wind of change. The ability to adapt to new trends, technologies, and business needs is what keeps the governance model from becoming obsolete.

Following the beacon of clarity, we encounter accountability. It's the principle that whispers, "With great power comes great responsibility." Ensuring that there are defined mechanisms for accountability throughout the contingent workforce management process is like having a compass that always points to true north. It helps in maintaining the integrity of the program, with each stakeholder understanding their role in the symphony of operations.

Then, we have the principle of inclusivity. Embrace it, and you'll see your program flourish like a well-tended garden. Inclusivity in governance means acknowledging and valuing the contributions of all stakeholders, including vendors, contingent workers, and internal teams. It's about creating a governance model that considers diverse perspectives, fostering an environment of collaboration and mutual respect.

Let's not forget the rhythm of regular reviews. Just like how seasons change, so do business environments. Regularly reviewing your governance framework and its outcomes ensures that your contingent workforce program remains relevant and responsive to evolving business needs and external factors. It's not merely an audit; it's a tune-up to ensure your governance engine runs smoothly.

Integral to robust governance is the practice of strategic communication. It's the lifeblood that maintains the heartbeat of your contingent workforce program. Effective communication strategies ensure that all parties are informed, engaged, and aligned with the program's objectives and changes. Remember, in the age of information, silence is often taken as inaction or, worse, ignorance.

Data-driven decision-making is the cornerstone of effective governance. By leveraging analytics, organizations can monitor key performance indicators (KPIs), assess compliance risks, and make informed decisions that optimize the management of contingent labor. Metrics such as contractor performance, time-to-hire, and compliance with local labor laws can provide critical insights, enabling proactive governance adjustments. Implementing an advanced Vendor Management System (VMS) or data analytics tool can automate this process, ensuring real-time access to crucial governance data. Where data is the new oil, leveraging analytical insights for governance decisions can remarkably enhance the efficacy and efficiency of your contingent workforce management. It's like having a crystal ball, but one grounded, providing insights into your program's health and guiding strategic decisions.

Risk management is an essential component of governance, acting as the safeguard against compliance failures, financial missteps, and reputational damage. A robust governance framework must include proactive risk identification, comprehensive assessment, and clear mitigation strategies. Implementing risk management protocols—such as regular audits, vendor reviews, and compliance checks—ensures that your program is equipped to navigate uncertainties and avoid costly mistakes. A robust governance framework incorporates proactive risk identification, assessment, and mitigation strategies, allowing your program to navigate through the stormy weathers of uncertainty with confidence.

Lastly, the principle of continuous improvement encourages a mindset of ongoing evolution and refinement. It's understood that perfection is not a destination but a journey. Encouraging feedback, learning from successes and failures alike, and being open to change, are the hallmarks of a governance model that not only endures but thrives.

In wrapping up, remember that robust governance is not about imposing rigid controls or bureaucracies. It's about creating a dynamic system that supports your contingent workforce program's goals, fosters transparency and trust, and adapts to the ever-changing business. It's about steering your contingent labor ship through both calm and turbulent waters with expertise, foresight, and a touch of grace.

As we move forward, bear in mind these principles and practices. They're not just guidelines; they're the gears that drive your program towards success, efficiency, and resilience. Just like mastering the art of making a perfect cup of coffee, getting governance right enriches your contingent workforce program, making it robust, responsive, and ready for the future.

Setting Standards and Ensuring Compliance

When it comes to the intricate world of contingent workforce management, one adage that certainly rings true is, "Good fences make good neighbors." This is a slightly cheeky way of saying that clear boundaries, or in our case, standards, and compliance frameworks, are not just necessary; they're foundational to the success and harmony of any contingent labor program. Now, let's roll up our sleeves and dive in, shall we?

Imagine for a moment that you're building a magnificent castle (your contingent labor program) in the middle of an ever-evolving landscape (the contingent workforce industry). The construction of this castle is guided by a set of blueprints (standards) to ensure it can withstand the tests of time and law (compliance). Without these blueprints, our castle might as well be made of cards, susceptible to the slightest puff of wind (legal repercussions, inefficiencies, etc.).

Standards in the contingent workforce realm are akin to the quality and safety guidelines that govern the construction of physical structures. They address everything from worker classification, payment terms, to the ethical treatment of workers. They provide a framework that helps ensure your program doesn't inadvertently become a rogue operation that flouts labor laws or treats its workers unjustly.

Ensuring compliance, on the other hand, is the process of regularly checking that the standards are not just written down but followed to the T. It's the architect visiting the construction site, making sure that the builders are not substituting gold for pyrite. And in the contingent workforce program, this could mean conducting audits, reviewing vendor practices, and keeping an eye on regulatory updates.

Now, one could argue that setting up standards and ensuring compliance sounds like an awful lot of work—and they wouldn't be wrong. But consider this: the price of non-compliance can be steep, ranging from legal battles that drain your coffers to damage to your reputation that can take years to mend. It's like realizing your castle has been built on a sinkhole; the repercussions could be disastrous.

Many companies have found that investing in a robust Vendor Management System (VMS) can be a game-changer for compliance. A VMS can act as the castle's vigilant sentinels, keeping an eye on vendor performances, worker classifications, and other critical metrics. They essentially automate much of the heavy lifting, making compliance less of a dreaded chore.

Let's also talk about the importance of building a culture of compliance within your organization. It's not just about having rules; it's about weaving those rules into the fabric of your everyday operations. When your team understands the 'why' behind the standards and compliance efforts, adherence becomes more natural than forced. It's about turning compliance from a box-ticking exercise into a way of life.

Engagement with legal counsel early and often cannot be overstated. The contingent workforce industry is a beast of its own when it comes to legal considerations, subject to differing laws and regulations across jurisdictions. Therefore, having legal counsel in your corner is like having a seasoned guide while navigating a labyrinth; it could save you from taking a wrong turn.

In the spirit of keeping up with the dynamism of the contingent workforce market, setting standards and ensuring compliance is not a "one and done" task. It's an ongoing endeavor. As the industry evolves, so must your approach to compliance. New types of worker classifications may emerge, and regulatory landscapes can shift. Staying informed and flexible is paramount.

Effective communication with your vendors and contractors is also essential in maintaining standards and compliance. It's not just about dictating terms but fostering a collaborative environment where compliance is a shared goal. After all, a chain is only as strong as its weakest link; ensuring your vendors are on the same page strengthens your program's integrity.

Considering the potential pitfalls of non-compliance, one might think setting up an internal task force dedicated to standards and compliance is the way to go. This unit could be responsible for staying abreast of legal changes, conducting audits, and facilitating training and education programs for both staff and vendors. Think of them as the castle's stewards, ensuring the fortress remains impregnable.

Training and continuous education play a crucial role in ensuring compliance. It's not enough to set up rules; you have to ensure that everyone involved in your contingent labor program understands them. Regular training sessions can help ensure that your staff, suppliers, and even the contingent workers themselves are aware of the expectations and the consequences of non-compliance.

To wrap up, setting standards and ensuring compliance in the realm of contingent workforce management might seem daunting, akin to herding cats at times. But with a methodical approach, the right tools, and an unwavering commitment to integrity, it's not only doable—it's essential. Just remember, at the heart of every successful contingent labor program is a solid foundation of standards and compliance. So, keep building your castle thoughtfully, and rest assured, it will stand the test of time.

In the next section, we'll explore the role of leadership in governance, because, as we all know, the tone at the top can significantly influence the culture of compliance and governance within an organization. But that's a story for another day. For now, let's keep our focus on ensuring our castles are built on solid ground.

Role of Leadership in Governance

In contingent workforce management, leaders are not just figureheads but navigators who steer the ship through both calm and stormy seas. Given the dynamic and often unpredictable nature of contingent labor, the role of leadership in governance cannot be overstated. It's like being the captain of a very flexible, yet occasionally unruly, pirate crew, where everyone has a unique skill set, and it's your job to keep all hands-on deck and moving in the same direction.

Firstly, it's crucial for leaders to have a clear vision. This vision provides the beacon of light guiding the strategies and policies related to contingent workforce governance. Without this, organizations run the risk of veering off course, potentially into the murky waters of non-compliance or mismanagement. Imagine trying to navigate a ship without a compass; that's a company without a clear goal in contingent workforce management.

Moreover, leadership in governance transcends traditional management roles. It involves championing the cause of contingent workers within the broader organizational context. This includes advocating for fair treatment, equitable opportunities, and inclusion in company culture. It's akin to ensuring every member of the pirate crew has a spot at the table, not just the first mates and quartermasters.

Effective leadership also means fostering an environment of transparency and accountability. Like the captain who must answer to the crew, leaders must communicate decisions and policies regarding contingent labor clearly and openly. This transparency builds trust and ensures that everyone is aware of the governance framework and their role within it.

Leaders must also be adept at navigating the regulatory landscape. Just as the seas are governed by international maritime laws, contingent workforce management is subject to a plethora of legal and compliance requirements. Staying ahead of these regulations, understanding their implications, and ensuring compliance are vital leadership responsibilities. Think of it as avoiding the metaphorical regulatory icebergs that could sink the ship.

In fostering collaboration, leaders in contingent workforce governance act as the bridge between permanent and contingent staff, ensuring integration and cohesion. It's about breaking down the us-versus-them mentality and promoting a unified team spirit, much like a captain ensuring harmony among the crew regardless of their roles or origins.

Leadership is also about setting standards. This goes beyond drafting policy documents; it's about embodying the principles of integrity, fairness, and excellence. Leaders must walk the talk, setting an example for others to follow. Just as a captain's conduct sets the tone onboard, a leader's behavior influences the organization's culture and governance practices.

Moreover, leaders play a crucial role in strategic planning and risk management. With the contingent workforce industry constantly developing, leaders must anticipate changes and devise strategies to mitigate risks. This requires not just insight, but foresight — the ability to look ahead and prepare for future challenges and opportunities.

Adaptability is another critical facet of leadership in governance. Just as a skilled captain adjusts the sails to meet the changing winds, leaders must be flexible in their approach to managing contingent labor. This means being open to new ideas, technologies, and strategies that can enhance efficiency and compliance.

Furthermore, communication is a leader's compass. Regular, clear, and effective communication helps ensure that everyone understands their roles, responsibilities, and the governance frameworks in place. It also fosters a culture of feedback, where contingent workers feel valued and heard.

Leaders should also advocate for technological adoption and innovation. In the age of digital transformation, leveraging technology can streamline processes, improve compliance, and enhance the overall management of the contingent workforce. It's about using every tool in the chest to keep the ship sailing smoothly.

Training and development play a significant role in governance, and leaders must champion these efforts. By providing training for both managers and contingent workers, organizations can ensure better compliance, performance, and integration. It's akin to equipping the crew with the skills and knowledge they need to navigate the high seas successfully.

In driving cultural change, leaders must embed the value of the contingent workforce within the organization's DNA. This means recognizing contingent workers not as outsiders but as integral members of the team who contribute to the organization's success. It's about changing perceptions and fostering a culture of inclusivity and respect.

Finally, leaders must continuously monitor and evaluate governance practices. This involves not just checking the compass but making adjustments to the course as needed. By regularly reviewing policies, processes, and performance, leaders can ensure that governance frameworks remain effective and aligned with organizational goals.

In the vast ocean of contingent workforce management, leadership is the rudder that guides the ship. Through vision, transparency, collaboration, and adaptability, leaders can navigate the complexities of governance, ensuring that their organization not only survives but thrives in the shifting tides of the contingent labor market.

Chapter 4: Vendor Neutrality in an MSP Contingent Workforce Program

Zooming in from our broad overview of contingent workforce program governance, we find ourselves peeking into the world of vendor neutrality – a centerpiece in the mosaic of Managed Service Provider (MSP) strategies. It's a simple concept, really, like choosing not to have a favorite child; you give each vendor an equal shot at winning your business, ensuring no undue preference taints your judgment or the fairness of the playing field. It's not about playing Switzerland and refusing to take sides; it's about ensuring that when you do pick a side, it's done with equity and wisdom. Vendor neutrality is the principle of offering all approved suppliers equal opportunities to provide services, without giving preference to any one vendor. This ensures that vendor selection is based purely on performance, quality, and cost-effectiveness, rather than relationships or historical affiliations. In the context of an MSP (Managed Service Provider) contingent workforce program, vendor neutrality creates an open, competitive environment where vendors are motivated to continually enhance their offerings. This not only fosters innovation but also drives down costs and ensures compliance with the organization's procurement policies.

Now, imagine a scene where every vendor is given a fair crack at the whip. Here we're not playing favorites; we're running a talent acquisition reality show where everyone's got talent, and the best performer wins. Implementing vendor neutrality starts with understanding the needs of your organization. This means clear criteria for selection, transparent processes, and open lines of communication. These are the nuts and bolts of managing vendor relationships. Yet, it's also about knowing when to step back and let the vendors show what they're made of. This delicate dance involves monitoring and evaluating vendor performance without preconceptions clouding your vision. It's like being a judge on that talent show – you might have a soft spot for magicians, but if the juggler throws their heart and soul into the performance, they deserve the accolade.

There are many opportunities that arise when we adopt a vendor neutrality approach. It not only ensures a diverse supply chain, but it also fosters innovation and creativity by motivating vendors to improve their performance. And while the execution of vendor neutrality might seem like balancing on a rope across a gap of confusion and compliance, the view from the center – seeing vendors develop solutions and candidates that align with our organization's culture and goals – is very impressive. So, here's to vendor neutrality: may our MSP contingent workforce programs be as diverse and dynamic as a well-planned wardrobe – full of surprises, but always on point.

Concept and Importance of Vendor Neutrality

The complex choreography of overseeing a flexible workforce relies on the key principle of vendor neutrality, which is essential for the success of the whole operation. This fundamental idea, ingrained in the Managed Service Provider (MSP) model, promotes fairness and objectivity, guaranteeing that every service provider — regardless of their scale or past projects — has the same opportunity to add their distinctive talents to the organizational mix.

As a cook in a huge food world, where you can get ingredients from many different suppliers, each supplier has different herbs and spices, some common and some unusual. Choosing vendor neutrality in this situation is like judging each ingredient only on its quality, how it fits your dish, instead of depending on your familiarity with certain suppliers. This way not only improves your food creations but also encourages innovation and diversity in your kitchen.

This example applies easily to the area of MSP and contingent workforce management. By practicing vendor neutrality, organizations make sure that the process of choosing vendors is as fair and objective as possible, like in a blind taste test. Vendor neutrality ensures that all suppliers compete on an even playing field, promoting the emergence of the best solutions based purely on merit. This competitive environment drives innovation among vendors, as they are motivated to continuously improve their offerings to secure contracts. Additionally, organizations benefit from cost savings as competitive pricing pressures vendors to offer better rates. Over time, vendor neutrality can lead to a higher quality of talent, as only the top-performing vendors remain in the program, leading to more efficient workforce management and higher contractor satisfaction.

Vendor neutrality has a direct and measurable impact on reducing costs within a Managed Service Provider (MSP) program. By ensuring that all vendors compete based on performance metrics and price, neutrality encourages vendors to offer their most competitive rates to secure contracts. This natural competition leads to cost savings by preventing inflated pricing that can occur when preferred vendors dominate the landscape.

Furthermore, because vendors are motivated to maintain high standards of service, organizations benefit from reduced rework costs, as higher-quality candidates lead to better long-term fits. With fewer project delays or contract disputes, organizations experience cost efficiencies across their entire contingent workforce. Vendor neutrality also prevents vendor monopolization, ensuring that no single vendor can increase rates due to a lack of competition.

Over time, these competitive pressures drive down total procurement costs, as vendors are incentivized to improve both pricing structures and service delivery to remain competitive. The result is a balanced ecosystem where organizations achieve the best value for their investment without sacrificing quality.

And vendors are acutely aware that their offerings are evaluated against a transparent, equitable benchmark, a natural competitive spirit is fostered. This competitive ecosystem not only potentially lowers costs through healthy bidding wars but also elevates the quality of services and talent presented to the organization.

The advantages of such an environment are manifold. With vendors striving to outdo each other within a fair and structured framework, organizations benefit from access to top-tier talent and innovative solutions. This competition breeds excellence, pushing vendors to constantly refine and improve their offerings to secure or retain their place within an organization's vendor roster.

Moreover, the implementation of vendor neutrality transcends the initial selection phase, embedding itself into the ongoing relationship between organizations and their vendors. Through the utilization of advanced Vendor Management Systems (VMS), the process remains transparent and unbiased, with technology acting as the impartial mediator that ensures continued adherence to the principles of vendor neutrality.

Achieving vendor neutrality is not without its challenges. One of the main difficulties is overcoming inherent biases that may exist due to long-standing relationships with certain vendors. Additionally, implementing a fully neutral approach can become complex when managing a global supply chain, where regional suppliers might have varying compliance standards and capabilities. Ensuring neutrality across such a diverse vendor pool requires robust systems that can evaluate vendors based on consistent performance metrics, regardless of geographical location. Moreover, change management plays a crucial role in shifting organizational culture away from legacy preferences toward a truly performance-driven approach. It demands a shift in organizational culture from one that might favor historical affiliations to a more objective, performance-driven approach. Leadership endorsement and advocacy for vendor neutrality are crucial, as it sets the expectation and standard for the entire contingent workforce management strategy.

Exploring vendor neutrality reveals its capacity to foster a diverse and vibrant supplier ecosystem. This diversity is not just superficial; it's a strategic asset that injects flexibility and innovation into the contingent workforce, enabling organizations to swiftly adapt to changing market dynamics and emerging opportunities.

The legal and compliance benefits of vendor neutrality also stand out. By ensuring that all vendors are evaluated and managed through a consistent, unbiased lens, organizations can better navigate the complex landscape of contractor classifications, regulatory compliance, and mitigate associated risks. This consistent approach safeguards against potential legal entanglements and reinforces the organization's commitment to ethical and fair practices.

Vendor neutrality also shifts the focus from merely winning contracts to excelling in performance and delivery. With a leveled competitive field, the emphasis naturally moves towards delivering exceptional results, fostering a culture of excellence and innovation among the vendor community. This performance-driven environment not only enhances the quality of work but also encourages vendors to continuously innovate and improve their services.

The flexibility inherent in vendor neutrality allows organizations to tailor their engagement strategies with vendors, ensuring that these strategies are aligned with specific needs and objectives. This adaptability is crucial, allowing organizations to navigate the evolving business landscape while maintaining a fair and competitive vendor ecosystem.

Vendor neutrality, at its heart, is more than a procurement strategy; it's a guiding philosophy that elevates fairness, encourages healthy competition, and champions innovation. It prompts organizations to venture beyond their comfort zones, exploring a rich array of vendor offerings that might otherwise remain overshadowed by pre-existing biases.

As we delve deeper into the nuances of implementing vendor neutrality, it's essential to approach this journey with an open mind, ready to explore and embrace the diverse offerings that lie within the vast vendor landscape. By adhering to the principles of vendor neutrality, organizations not only enhance their operational excellence but also contribute to a more equitable, innovative, and dynamic contingent workforce ecosystem.

In summary, vendor neutrality is not just a component of a successful MSP Contingent Workforce Program; it is the cornerstone upon which ethical, efficient, and effective vendor engagements are built. It challenges traditional procurement paradigms, advocating for a system where quality, innovation, and fairness prevail. As we progress, the essence of vendor neutrality—emphasizing fairness, fostering competition, and prioritizing quality—becomes instrumental in revolutionizing contingent workforce management, setting a new standard for excellence in the field.

Implementing Vendor Neutrality

When it comes to setting the stage for a vendor-neutral Managed Service Provider (MSP) contingent workforce program, one might liken the approach to organizing a potluck dinner. You're aiming for a spread that's diverse and inclusive, ensuring no single dish overshadows another, and each vendor gets a fair shake at the table. The essence of implementing vendor neutrality in an MSP program isn't just about fairness; it's about leveraging the best talents and services on the market, ensuring the quality and cost-effectiveness of your contingent workforce.

Implementing vendor neutrality starts with creating a structured, unbiased vendor selection process. This means establishing clear, data-driven criteria for vendor evaluation, which should focus on performance metrics such as time-to-fill, candidate quality, cost-efficiency, and compliance with labor laws. Advanced Vendor Management Systems (VMS) can automate much of this process, ensuring that each vendor is evaluated based on objective, quantifiable data rather than subjective factors. VMS platforms can also enforce transparency by providing real-time analytics on vendor performance, helping organizations maintain neutrality throughout the engagement process. Picture starting with a clean slate every time, where decisions are driven by data and performance metrics, not by handshakes and goodwill. It's a funny thing, really; how often the biggest decisions boil down to the simple mechanics of who can deliver on time, on budget, and above expectations. Implementing a scoring system based on these criteria can transform the selection process from a subjective guessing game into an objective competition that brings the best to the forefront.

Communication, as in any relationship, is key. Keeping every vendor in the loop, from the expectations to the feedback process, is crucial. It's like hosting a game night and making sure everyone knows the rules before they start playing. This openness fosters a transparent environment where vendors are motivated to compete fairly and are continually informed about where they stand. Regular performance reviews and an open-door feedback mechanism ensure that vendors are not left in the dark, pondering their fate like contestants on a reality show but are partners moving towards a common goal.

Technological integration cannot be overlooked. In a world that's increasingly digital, having the right Vendor Management System (VMS) in place can be a game-changer. Think of it as the digital referee that ensures everyone plays by the rules. A robust VMS can automate the bidding and selection process, enforce compliance, and provide insightful analytics, thereby reducing manual oversight and the potential for bias. Vendor Management Systems (VMS) are critical to enforcing vendor neutrality by acting as the central technology platform through which all vendor interactions are managed. A VMS ensures that each vendor is evaluated based on objective performance criteria, eliminating the risk of favoritism. Through automation, VMS platforms streamline the vendor selection process by tracking key performance indicators (KPIs) such as **time-to-fill**, **quality of hire**, and **cost per placement**. The system aggregates this data into a transparent dashboard, allowing decision-makers to compare vendors on equal footing.

Additionally, a VMS enhances compliance by automatically flagging any deviations from established policies, such as vendor overuse or violations of contractual terms. By providing real-time analytics, it also allows organizations to monitor vendor performance continually, ensuring that only the best-performing suppliers are rewarded with future opportunities. With this level of transparency and automation, a VMS reinforces the integrity of vendor neutrality while reducing the administrative burden on procurement teams.

Really, implementing vendor neutrality isn't just adopting a set of rules; it's embracing a philosophy. It's about recognizing that in the rich tapestry that is the contingent workforce, each thread—no matter how seemingly insignificant—can add value to the bigger picture. By fostering an environment where every vendor has an equal opportunity to shine, organizations can not only ensure the quality and diversity of their contingent workforce but can also drive innovation and competitive advantage in an ever-evolving marketplace.

Managing Vendor Relationships

Let's dive into the art and science of managing vendor relationships within the MSP Contingent Workforce Program. Picture this: your organization is a bustling metropolis, and your vendors are the bridges connecting you to the diverse talent islands scattered across the vast ocean of the contingent workforce. Managing these bridges effectively is pivotal. It's not just about ensuring they're sturdy and reliable, but also about making them avenues of mutual growth and understanding.

First things first, open and transparent communication is the golden key in this quest. It's astonishing how many potential pitfalls can be avoided by simply keeping the lines of dialogue open. This ensures that expectations are set, feedback is given timely, and any issues are addressed proactively rather than reactively.

Second on our list is the concept of trust, but verify. Trust in your vendors plays a foundational role in building strong relationships. However, complementing this trust with regular reviews and assessments ensures that the quality of work meets your evolving business needs. It's like having a safety net in place, just in case.

Equally important, is understanding the value of strategic alignment. Ensure that your vendors are not just aware of your immediate requirements but are also in tune with your long-term business goals. This alignment is critical for fostering a partnership that can dynamically adapt as your business evolves.

Let's not forget the importance of recognizing and celebrating success. When a vendor surpasses your expectations or goes the extra mile, acknowledge it. These gestures of appreciation can significantly bolster motivation and dedication, driving a deeper commitment to your business's success.

Now, onto the delicate dance of negotiations. It's imperative to approach these discussions with a win-win mindset. Fair and balanced agreements pave the way for a more robust and enduring partnership. Think of it as building a bridge sturdy enough to withstand the test of time.

How about innovation? Encourage your vendors to bring forward new ideas and solutions. This not just keeps your services on the cutting edge but also signals to your vendors that their input is valued and that they play a crucial role in your business's growth.

Let's also talk about vendor diversity. Embracing a mix of vendors, including small and minority-owned businesses, can enrich your vendor ecosystem with fresh perspectives and solutions, potentially opening new avenues for innovation and improvement.

Performance metrics, undoubtedly, are your compass in this journey. Establish clear, measurable goals for vendors to achieve. This not only gives them a target to aim for but also helps you evaluate their performance objectively.

In the realm of challenges, conflict resolution mechanisms cannot be overstated. Despite best efforts, disputes will arise. Having a clear, fair, and predetermined process for resolving disagreements protects both your interests and those of your vendors.

On to partnership development - treat your vendors as partners rather than mere suppliers. This paradigm shift from a transactional relationship to a partnership fosters a more cohesive and productive working environment, where shared goals take precedence.

Don't overlook the role of technology in managing these relationships. Vendor Management Systems (VMS) can streamline processes, offer real-time insights, and facilitate better communication. It's like having a high-tech bridge with all the bells and whistles to ensure smooth operations.

Another critical aspect is risk management. Regularly assess the risks involved in your vendor relationships and work collaboratively to mitigate them. This not only protects your business but also ensures that your vendors are operating sustainably and responsibly.

Continually educate and train your vendors on your business processes, compliance requirements, and operational standards. This ensures they are well-equipped to meet your needs and reduces the learning curve, leading to more efficient service delivery.

Last but certainly not least, stay informed about industry trends and benchmarks. This knowledge enables you to set realistic expectations, identify opportunities for improvement, and keep your vendor relationships aligned with industry best practices.

Managing vendor relationships within the MSP Contingent Workforce Program is akin to being an accomplished conductor of an orchestra. It requires a nuanced understanding of each vendor's unique capabilities and challenges, as well as the skill to harmonize these diverse elements into a symphony that propels your business forward. By embracing these principles, you can transform your vendor relationships from mere transactions into strategic partnerships that drive mutual success.

Monitoring and Evaluating Vendor Performance

As we delve into the intricacies of managing vendor relationships within a MSP contingent workforce program, it's paramount to remember that monitoring and evaluating vendor performance isn't just a checkbox exercise. It's about nurturing a dynamic, responsive, and ultimately profitable partnership. Think of it as a dance. Sometimes it's a tango, intense and precise; other times, it's more of a cha-cha, with quick steps forward and backward, but always moving towards greater synergy and performance.

Monitoring vendor performance begins with setting clear, measurable benchmarks that align with both your company's strategic goals and specific workforce needs. Key performance indicators (KPIs) might include candidate quality scores, time-to-fill positions, compliance rates, cost per hire, and retention rates. Regular performance reviews should be scheduled to assess these metrics and identify areas where vendors may need to improve. Additionally, organizations can use VMS platforms to generate performance dashboards, providing real-time visibility into vendor effectiveness and ensuring accountability. And you know what? Sometimes, benchmarks need a good old reality check. Because setting the bar at an Olympic high jump height for a game of limbo is just setting everyone up for failure.

Regular performance evaluations are key. It's not about playing gotcha with the vendors but engaging them in a constructive dialogue where feedback goes both ways. Trust me, vendors aren't mind readers (although, wouldn't that make things easier?), and without candid feedback, they can't rectify issues or adapt to your evolving needs. These evaluations can also highlight potential areas for innovation and growth, turning a routine check-in into a brainstorming session for future successes.

Data plays a starring role in this process. With the right metrics, you can track everything from cost-effectiveness to compliance, quality of work, and timeliness. It's like having a fitness tracker for your vendor relationships – it tells you where things are going smoothly and where you might need to put in a bit more effort.

However, it's not just about collecting data. It's about understanding what that data tells us. This is where vendor management systems (VMS) strut onto the stage. A robust VMS can provide analytics that make sense of the numbers, offering insights that can lead to informed decisions and strategic adjustments. Think of it as the difference between reading tea leaves and having a crystal ball.

And let's not forget about the power of relationships. At the end of the day, vendor partnerships are built on trust and collaboration. It's through regular, open communication that issues can be preemptively addressed, and opportunities for mutual growth can be seized. Imagine it as crafting a bespoke suit; you're constantly adjusting and fine-tuning until you've got something that fits perfectly.

Inclusive in this ongoing dialogue should be the discussion about value. It's essential to look beyond the invoices and understand the value added by each vendor. This could be in innovation, market knowledge, or even stability they bring to your supply chain. Realizing and recognizing this value can transform a transactional relationship into a strategic partnership.

Risk management is another critical component. Evaluating vendor performance also means assessing their ability to respond to and recover from risks. This resilience is crucial, especially in today's volatile market conditions. It's somewhat like having a sturdy umbrella in a storm; you want to make sure it won't turn inside out at the first gust of wind.

Establishing a performance improvement plan (PIP) when vendors don't meet expectations is also important. It's not about doling out penalties but working together to identify root causes and solutions. This is where creativity can flourish, as you and your vendors brainstorm innovative ways to overcome challenges and improve performance.

Feedback should go both ways. Just as you evaluate your vendors, invite them to provide feedback on your processes and approach. This two-way street can lead to improvements on both sides, enhancing the overall partnership. It's akin to sharing a road trip playlist; everyone gets to contribute their favorite tunes, resulting in a journey that's enjoyable for all.

Celebrating successes together is just as important. Recognizing and highlighting when vendors go above and beyond not only fosters a positive relationship but also sets the stage for future performance. It's the professional equivalent of giving a standing ovation; it acknowledges hard work and encourages even greater efforts in the future.

Lastly, maintaining a balance between flexibility and consistency is crucial. While it's important to adapt to changes and be flexible in approaches, there also needs to be a consistent framework for evaluating performance. This ensures fairness and objectivity in the process, akin to playing a game with clear rules where everyone knows how to score.

Monitoring and evaluating vendor performance in a MSP contingent workforce program is a multifaceted endeavor. It involves setting clear benchmarks, leveraging data, fostering strong relationships, managing risks, and celebrating successes. By approaching this process with a balance of humor, persuasion, and exposition, we can navigate the challenges and opportunities it presents, leading to a thriving ecosystem of vendors that contribute significantly to our strategic goals. So let's keep dancing the dance, tuning the performance, and maybe, just maybe, making the complex world of vendor management a little more harmonious.

Chapter 5: Understanding Vendor Management Systems (VMS)

We need to have a serious discussion about Vendor Management Systems (VMS). Imagine this: You have a jigsaw puzzle spread out in front of you. This puzzle? It's your contingent workforce management process. Now, I can almost sense the collective groan; managing a contingent workforce can feel like you're trying to control a bunch of bees in a jar—difficult and prone to getting out of your control. That's where the VMS comes in, your very own beekeeper's suit, designed to make managing those busy projects and freelancers easy. Let's explore how a VMS works not only as a protective layer but also as an organizational wizard.

At its core, a VMS is not just software; it's a strategic chameleon. It can adapt, reshape, and fit itself snugly into the contours of your business needs. A Vendor Management System (VMS) acts as a centralized platform that automates and streamlines the entire lifecycle of a contingent workforce. From requisition to invoicing, a VMS ensures that every step is efficient, compliant, and transparent. Think of a VMS as a sophisticated conductor for your contingent workforce orchestra, harmonizing the interaction between hiring managers, vendors, and contractors.

Beyond administrative efficiency, VMS solutions play a strategic role by providing real-time analytics, allowing organizations to monitor spend, vendor performance, and compliance with labor regulations. By consolidating this data, the VMS enables organizations to make data-driven decisions that enhance overall productivity and mitigate risks. It is the ultimate guardian of compliance, ensuring that every contractor and vendor follows corporate policies and labor laws. This regulatory oversight minimizes the risk of costly legal penalties and reputational damage.

From requisition to payment, a VMS streamlines the sourcing, engagement, management, and analysis of your contingent workforce. Consider the rhetorical question: Can you imagine a world where all your contingent workforce data—spending, compliance, performance metrics—is scattered like autumn leaves? Neither can I. That's the chaos a VMS saves you from. It consolidates this data, offering insights and oversight that would make even the most skeptical executive let out a low whistle of appreciation.

Now, selecting a VMS is akin to choosing a dance partner; you want one that matches your rhythm and pace. This process can feel like navigating a maze littered with technical jargon and sales pitches. However, fear not! Focusing on functionality, integration capabilities, vendor support, and cost can illuminate your path to finding a VMS that not only meets but gyrates seamlessly with your organization's unique needs. Whether it's automating timesheets or synthesizing financial reports, the right VMS will have you doing the management tango with ease.

But wait, there's more to VMS than meets the eye. Beyond its role as a formidable data aggregator and process streamliner, a VMS fosters collaboration and transparency across the board. It breaks down silos, allowing managers, suppliers, and contractors to waltz together in harmony. Communication barriers dissolve, and suddenly, you're not just managing a contingent workforce; you're nurturing a contingent community—a veritable hive of collective efficiency and innovation.

As we conclude this section, it's important to recognize that implementing a VMS is no simple fix. It demands strategic planning, patience, and a focus on change management. However, the outcomes—seamless efficiency, data-driven insights, and enhanced control—make the effort more than worthwhile. By fully understanding and leveraging the power of a VMS, you position yourself not just as part of the evolving contingent workforce landscape, but as a leader, ready to orchestrate a well-tuned operation of success.

Functions and Features of a VMS

It's obvious by now that managing a contingent workforce can be like trying to juggle while riding a unicycle—difficult, requires balance, and honestly, it's not something you learn overnight. That's where the Vendor Management System (VMS) comes in, the unsung hero for talent consultants, contingent workforce leaders, and companies diving into the contingent labor pool. A VMS is more than a tool; it's your virtual assistant designed to make life easier, tracking every contingent workforce detail while you focus on not dropping the ball.

A VMS is a system that handles the basic but important tasks of managing temporary workers. It's like having a very reliable personal assistant who works 24/7. This system deals with job requests, simplifies the application process, and organizes assignments among different vendors. Automation is the main feature—saving time in filling positions and making sure that talent sourcing is as easy as possible.

And what's a superhero without their gadgets?

Data analytics and reporting features in a VMS can make Batman's utility belt seem outdated. These tools provide real-time insights into spending, contractor performance, and program compliance. In a world where data is crucial, having these analytics at your disposal enables more informed decision-making and strategic planning, ensuring that your contingent workforce program always stays on track. Beyond standard data analytics, the integration of artificial intelligence (AI) within a VMS enhances decision-making by automating complex processes such as talent matching, workforce forecasting, and market trend predictions. AI algorithms can assess large volumes of data to recommend the best-fit candidates for open positions, shortening hiring cycles. Furthermore, machine learning embedded in the system refines recruitment criteria over time, improving the quality of talent selected by learning from past performance data. Predictive analytics provided by AI-driven VMS platforms can also forecast future workforce needs based on historical hiring patterns, helping organizations proactively manage their contingent workforce strategy.

Compliance risks can be as tricky to navigate as a minefield. However, with a VMS, companies can maintain their cool. It monitors contractor compliance with labor laws and corporate policies, reducing the risk of financial penalties or reputational damage. Like having a legal eagle in your pocket, it ensures that every "i" is dotted and every t is crossed.

Diversity spending tracking is another feather in the VMS cap. In our progressively inclusive world, supporting diversity is not just nice-to-have but a must-do. A VMS tracks spending with diverse suppliers, helping organizations meet their diversity goals and, in turn, enrich their corporate citizenship and brand reputation.

Scalability is a key topic in business, because if you're not growing, you're stagnating. A VMS can increase its functionality as your contingent workforce program develops, making sure that it is as agile and versatile as a Cirque du Soleil performer. A truly scalable VMS should not only accommodate current workforce needs but also be flexible enough to manage future growth. As your organization expands—whether that involves onboarding new suppliers, managing additional contingent roles, or entering new markets—the VMS must be able to adjust without requiring significant additional manual work. This might include **modular expansions** like integrating new compliance regulations, multi-country payroll capabilities, or handling larger pools of pre-vetted talent. The scalability of a VMS ensures that it evolves alongside the business, supporting operational complexity while maintaining efficiency. Whether it's adding new suppliers or including more contingent roles, a VMS adjusts to suit your needs.

A VMS excels at making onboarding and offboarding contractors hassle-free, like a perfect cup of coffee. It handles onboarding tasks, such as background checks and contract signing, and also takes care of offboarding, retrieving company assets and removing system access without any problems.

Cost management, an aspect as crucial as any, is adeptly handled by a VMS. It provides visibility into every cent spent on contingent labor, uncovers cost-saving opportunities, and helps enforce budget conformance. Essentially, it ensures that your financial health doesn't suffer while you leverage the talents of a diverse, agile workforce.

Speaking of agility, a VMS promotes vendor neutrality, ensuring that all suppliers are given a fair shot at filling job requisitions. This levels the playing field and fosters a competitive environment that can lead to better quality candidates and potentially lower costs. Vendor neutrality is a game-changer for cost management. By ensuring that all vendors have equal opportunities to fulfill job requisitions, a VMS promotes healthy competition. This level playing field drives higher-quality candidate submissions while also creating a competitive bidding environment that pushes down costs. Vendors, knowing they are being evaluated based on performance and cost efficiency, are motivated to offer competitive rates and improved services to secure contracts.

This dynamic ensures organizations avoid overpaying for talent, while still securing top-tier suppliers. Through the consistent enforcement of vendor neutrality, companies achieve both cost savings and high-quality workforce management without favoritism. Over time, this fosters a cost-effective vendor ecosystem where innovation and quality are prioritized. It's like ensuring every player gets to bat, regardless of the team they play for.

The communication capabilities within a VMS shouldn't be overlooked either. By centralizing communication, it keeps everyone, from hiring managers to suppliers, in the loop and on the same page. This eradicates the classic "left-hand doesn't know what the right hand is doing" scenario, promoting harmony and efficiency.

Integration features of a VMS are akin to a Swiss Army knife, offering the versatility to connect with other HR systems, procurement software, or ERP systems. This interoperability eliminates data silos and fosters a cohesive technology ecosystem, streamlining processes across the board. A VMS must seamlessly integrate with existing enterprise systems, such as HR management systems, enterprise resource planning (ERP) platforms, and procurement software. The ability to transfer data across these platforms without manual intervention ensures smoother workflows, reduces redundant data entry, and enhances data accuracy. This integration provides a consolidated view of contingent workforce operations across departments, which improves visibility into costs, compliance, and performance metrics. Whether it's enabling automated invoicing through ERP or syncing workforce data with HR platforms for seamless contractor management, effective integration eliminates bottlenecks and improves operational efficiency across the organization.

Talent pooling is another noteworthy function. A VMS can maintain a pool of pre-vetted candidates, ready to be tapped into whenever a need arises. This not only accelerates the hiring process but ensures that the talent well never runs dry, no matter the season.

But what about those looking to really drill down into the nitty-gritty? Rate management functionalities within a VMS allow for negotiation and standardization of contractor rates, ensuring that companies remain competitive while also fair to their contingent workforce. It's not just about keeping costs in check; it's about fostering a competitive yet equitable ecosystem that benefits all parties involved. By aligning contractor rates with market standards through informed negotiation, organizations not only ensure their competitive edge but also demonstrate fairness and commitment to their contingent workforce. In essence, it ensures everyone gets a fair shake, from the corporation down to the talent.

Finally, user experience is also important in a VMS. These systems are designed to be intuitive, so that anyone can use them easily and effectively, whether they are beginners or experts. After all, a tool is not useful if it's hard to figure out.

Therefore, don't be discouraged by the challenge of managing a contingent workforce, even if it seems as hard as climbing Everest in flip-flops. Think of a solid VMS as having the best equipment, assistance, and plan for your journey. It's about making the journey not only feasible but enjoyable. With the various functions and features designed to simplify, improve, and enrich your contingent workforce program, a VMS is more than a good idea; it's an essential strategy for keeping up in today's fast-moving, talent-driven market.

Selecting the Right VMS for Your Organization

When it's time to pick a Vendor Management System (VMS) for your organization, you might feel a bit like you're at a buffet with too many choices and not enough plate. It's crucial, though, because the right VMS can feel like having an extra set of hands managing your contingent workforce program, whereas the wrong choice can turn your program into a plate-spinning act where you're constantly one misstep away from disaster.

First things first, let's lay out what we're looking for. A VMS should not just be a tool; it ought to be your ally in the bustling world of contingent workforce management. Think of it like choosing a companion for a journey through the thickets of contingent labor management. You want someone reliable, who speaks your language, understands your goals, and, ideally, can tell a good joke now and then.

Understanding your organization's specific needs is the cornerstone of selecting the right VMS. It's tempting to go for the most feature-rich platform, but it's akin to buying a Swiss Army knife when all you need is a screwdriver. Start by mapping out your requirements. Do you need robust analytics, seamless integration with existing HR systems, or perhaps, a user-friendly interface is top of your list? Prioritize these needs because, in the VMS world, one size doesn't fit all.

The scalability of a VMS is paramount. Your organization isn't static; it's a living, breathing entity that grows, shifts, and changes direction. Your chosen VMS should be like a good pair of jeans - flexible enough to accommodate growth and changes in your workforce management strategy.

Integration capabilities can't be overlooked. The best VMS for your organization plays well with others, meaning it integrates seamlessly with your existing software ecosystems. If it demands too many bespoke adjustments or stands like an awkward outsider at a party, it's probably not the one.

Do consider the user experience (UX). A VMS that's as complicated as assembling furniture with instructions in a foreign language will only lead to frustration. You want a platform that's intuitive, engaging, and doesn't require a PhD in cryptology to understand. Remember, your users will range from your HR department to the managers making day-to-day contingent staffing decisions.

Don't skimp on support and training. Even the most intuitive VMS will have a learning curve, and you want a vendor that treats your success as their own. This means comprehensive onboarding, responsive customer support, and ongoing training resources to ensure your team gets the most out of the system.

Cost, while not the only consideration, is certainly a critical one. However, think of it as an investment rather than an expense. The cheapest option might save you some dollars upfront but cost you dearly in functionality and effectiveness down the line. Aim for the best value - the most bang for your buck, if you will.

Security features are non-negotiable. In an era where data breaches are more common than we'd like to admit, ensuring your VMS has top-notch security measures is imperative. After all, it will be handling sensitive information like contractor details, payment information, and potentially even intellectual property.

Vendor reputation and longevity are like the cherry on top. A vendor that has been around the block, has a strong track record, and is known for continuous improvement and innovation is more likely to be a reliable partner in your contingent workforce management journey.

Feedback from current users can offer invaluable insights. Look for reviews, case studies, and testimonials. It's like peeking into the future to see how your relationship with the VMS might unfold. And if possible, speak directly to current users. They can offer a depth of insight no brochure or sales pitch can match.

Finally, consider the analytics and reporting capabilities. The ability to turn data into actionable insights is what separates a good VMS from a great one. You should be able to easily report on spending, compliance, vendor performance, and other critical metrics.

Choosing the right VMS isn't just about ticking boxes; it's about finding a match for your organization's unique needs, culture, and goals. It's a bit like dating – you might have to spend some time getting to know each other before you commit. But when you find the right one, it can transform your contingent workforce management from a challenge into a strategic advantage.

Selecting the right VMS for your organization is a critical decision that requires careful consideration of your unique needs, scalability, integration capabilities, UX, support and training, cost, security features, vendor reputation, user feedback, and analytics and reporting capabilities. With the right partner, managing your contingent workforce can become a seamless, efficient part of your broader talent strategy, laying a foundation for flexibility and innovation in the face of changing business industries.

Take your time, do your research, and choose wisely. The future of your contingent workforce program depends on it. And remember, in the world of VMS, the best choice is not about having all the bells and whistles; it's about finding the right tool that aligns with your journey. Happy hunting!

Chapter 6: Differentiating MSP and Internal PMO

After covering the vital sectors of Vendor Management Systems and how they help you manage your flexible workforce, let's switch to a topic that often causes confusion and maybe some nervousness. We're talking about cracking the code of the mysterious acronyms that many in the industry use daily - MSP and Internal PMO. As baffling as they may be, understanding the differences between a Managed Service Provider (MSP) and an Internal Project Management Office (PMO) is like knowing whether you're drinking an aged Bordeaux or a strong Napa Cabernet. Both have their role, but boy, the context matters.

Starting with the MSP, this external entity is your go-to orchestra conductor, ensuring each section of the contingent workforce symphony plays in harmony. They're the outside experts stepping in to manage your contingent workforce program, wielding their baton to direct recruitment, compliance, and performance monitoring. A Managed Service Provider (MSP) is responsible for providing expert guidance and operational management of the contingent workforce. They leverage extensive relationships with staffing vendors to provide strategic sourcing, ensuring that organizations access the right talent at the right time, while also managing costs. MSPs also ensure compliance with employment laws and corporate regulations, reducing risk for organizations. Additionally, they offer analytics and reporting that allow organizations to gain valuable insights into workforce performance and optimize operations. MSPs bring in technology, often through a VMS, which automates processes like requisition management, onboarding, time tracking, and invoicing, streamlining operations and minimizing errors. It's a bit like having a personal shopper for talent; they know the market inside out, have an array of suppliers at their fingertips, and aim to streamline your processes and cut costs where they can.

Conversely, the internal Program Management Office (PMO) is like having an in-house master chef capable of concocting gourmet dishes tailored to your tastes. This model focuses on leveraging internal resources to manage the contingent workforce. An internal PMO provides an in-house team dedicated to overseeing contingent workforce programs. This office applies project governance frameworks to ensure that all processes align with organizational standards and strategic goals. Unlike MSPs, which typically focus on external expertise and vendor management, the PMO is deeply ingrained in the organization's culture and operational practices. This allows for a more tailored approach, with the PMO team managing everything from resource allocation and performance monitoring to risk management. Internal PMOs often use data-driven insights to enhance decision-making and continuously refine processes to ensure that workforce goals are met efficiently. It involves forming a dedicated team within the organization that oversees the contingent labor program, blending strategic planning, governance, and execution. The taste of self-reliance in managing talent can be delicious but requires a certain palate for complexity and the capacity to handle intricate operational details.

Peeling back the layers, one might wonder, "Which is better? The MSP that brings external prowess and efficiency to the table or the Internal PMO that offers control and customized oversight?" It's a bit like asking if you'd prefer flying first-class or piloting your private jet - both have their allure. The MSP model shines in its ability to offer scalability, access to industry-specific expertise, and often, more robust technological infrastructures. However, don't underestimate the power of the Internal PMO. Its strengths lie in fostering a deeper alignment with organizational culture, offering direct control over contingent workforce management, and possibly engendering a more nuanced understanding of company-specific needs and goals.

Ultimately, deciding between an MSP and an Internal PMO isn't about finding a one-size-fits-all solution but understanding the unique needs and capabilities of your organization. Maybe your contingent workforce strategy calls for the bespoke attention an Internal PMO can offer. Or perhaps, the scalability and external expertise of an MSP fit your evolving needs like a glove. Whichever you lean towards, remember, it's not just about managing talent but mastering the art of blending strategic foresight with execution excellence. And on this journey of discovery, whether you decide to dine in or order out, the goal remains the same - a perfectly managed contingent workforce that drives your business forward.

MSP vs. PMO: Roles and Responsibilities

When it comes to managing a contingent workforce, companies often find themselves at a crossroads, choosing between an MSP (Managed Service Provider) or an internal PMO (Project Management Office). The decision isn't one to be taken lightly, and understanding the roles and responsibilities of each is like learning to navigate a city you thought you knew, but suddenly there are new roads, and some of the old ones are now one way.

An MSP serves as an external partner, specializing in managing a company's contingent workforce program. Think of them as the all-knowing guides in the uncharted territory of contingent hiring. Their expertise lies in vendor management, compliance, candidate sourcing, onboarding, and performance evaluation. It's their bread and butter to ensure your contingent workforce strategy aligns brilliantly with your business objectives.

The roles of an MSP might include:

1. **Strategic Sourcing and Procurement:** MSPs are instrumental in sourcing and procuring contingent labor across various disciplines, leveraging extensive networks and relationships with staffing vendors. They implement strategic sourcing techniques to ensure quality talent acquisition at competitive rates, optimizing the workforce according to project demands and market dynamics.

2. **Vendor Management and Compliance:** A core function of MSPs is managing multiple staffing vendors, ensuring compliance with legal requirements, organizational policies, and industry standards. They standardize contracts, negotiate terms, and conduct performance evaluations, streamlining vendor interactions to reduce complexity and risk.

3. **Workforce Analytics and Optimization:** MSPs utilize advanced analytics to offer insights into workforce composition, cost, and performance metrics. This data-driven approach enables organizations to make informed decisions, identify trends, and anticipate future workforce needs, ensuring optimal resource allocation and operational efficiency.

4. **Risk Management:** They proactively identify, assess, and mitigate risks associated with contingent labor, including compliance with labor laws, co-employment issues, and data security, safeguarding the organization against potential legal and financial exposures.

Responsibilities:

- Implementing technology solutions, such as Vendor Management Systems (VMS), to automate and streamline processes.

- Fostering a competitive vendor environment to ensure the best value and service quality.

- Providing continuous improvement strategies based on performance data and market trends.

- Ensuring a seamless integration of contingent workers into the organization's culture and operational model.

An internal PMO is the in-house expertise. This group or office within your organization concentrates on managing and delivering program quality, including those that involve temporary workers. The PMO gives an insider's view on the company's program, rather than the external outlook of an MSP, making sure that resources are allocated optimally and appropriately to achieve program-specific objectives.

The roles of an PMO might include:

1. **Program Governance and Standards:** The PMO establishes and maintains project management standards and methodologies, ensuring consistency and quality in program execution. It acts as the custodian of best practices, governance frameworks, and compliance with regulatory requirements, enhancing project outcomes and alignment with strategic objectives.

2. **Performance Measurement:** The PMO is responsible for tracking and measuring project performance against

defined metrics and KPIs. It provides executive oversight, monitoring progress, budget adherence, and quality standards, facilitating timely interventions to keep any projects on track.

3. **Knowledge Management and Capacity Building:** It fosters a culture of learning and continuous improvement by capturing lessons learned, facilitating knowledge sharing, and developing program management competencies within the organization. The PMO plays a key role in building project management capacity and enhancing organizational maturity.

Responsibilities:

- Guiding managers and teams through the program's lifecycle, offering tools, templates, and expertise.

- Facilitating stakeholder communication and reporting, ensuring transparency and alignment.

- Identifying and addressing project risks and issues, providing strategic direction and support.

- Promoting innovation and strategic thinking within project teams, driving value creation and competitive advantage.

Integrating the roles of MSP and PMO can create a cohesive framework for managing not only the contingent workforce but also the projects and initiatives they support. While the MSP focuses on the operational and tactical aspects of contingent workforce management, the PMO provides strategic oversight and governance for projects. Together, they can ensure that an organization's contingent workforce is aligned with its strategic objectives, projects are executed efficiently, and resources are optimized across the board.

MSP and PMO can work together to increase organizational flexibility, boost project and workforce results, and gain an edge over rivals in today's changing business landscape. By learning and using the distinct functions and duties of each, organizations can adopt a comprehensive method to contingent workforce and program management, creating opportunities for innovation, growth, and success.

Pros and Cons of Each Model

Deciding between an MSP or an internal PMO depends largely on your organization's specific needs and strategic priorities. MSPs excel in providing scalability and external expertise, often reducing the burden on internal teams. They bring cost-efficiency through economies of scale and offer advanced workforce analytics capabilities, but organizations may feel they have less direct control over contingent workforce management. On the other hand, an Internal PMO offers more control and alignment with company culture, but it requires significant internal resources and expertise to manage effectively. PMOs may also have limited access to external networks and industry-specific knowledge compared to MSPs.

Dealing with a flexible workforce can be complicated, and we can contrast the MSP model with the internal PMO. Both have advantages and disadvantages, like choosing between a versatile tool and a specialized kitchen knife. The best option largely depends on the kind of business needs and preferences, metaphorically speaking.

To understand how engagement strategies affect a contingent

workforce, we need to use multiple measures that show not only immediate results but also long-term impacts on organizational goals and workforce integration. The following metrics are crucial in evaluating the effectiveness of engagement strategies:

Worker Satisfaction and Engagement Scores

- **Metric Overview:** Utilize surveys and feedback mechanisms to measure contingent workers' contentment and engagement levels regarding their roles, work environment, and interactions within the organization.

- **Why It Matters:** High satisfaction and engagement indicate a positive culture and effective communication, crucial for productivity and retention.

- **Measuring Tips:** Implement regular, anonymous surveys focusing on key areas of engagement and satisfaction. Use Likert scales for nuanced responses and include open-ended questions for qualitative insights.

Project Completion Rates and Quality

- **Metric Overview:** Analyze project timelines, completion rates against deadlines, and adherence to quality standards.

- **Why It Matters:** Successful engagement correlates with on-time, high-quality project completions, underscoring effective alignment and motivation among contingent workers.

- **Measuring Tips:** Track project milestones, use client or stakeholder feedback for quality assessment, and benchmark against industry standards or historical data for continuous improvement.

Retention and Turnover Rates

- **Metric Overview:** Track turnover and retention specifically among contingent workers within the organization.

- **Why It Matters:** Lower turnover and higher retention suggest that engagement strategies are effectively making contingent roles rewarding and growth oriented.

- **Measuring Tips:** Analyze retention rates in relation to industry averages and investigate exit interview data for turnover insights, identifying areas for engagement strategy enhancements.

Time-to-Productivity

- **Metric Overview:** Measure the average duration for new contingent workers to achieve full productivity post-onboarding.

- **Why It Matters:** A reduced time-to-productivity signifies efficient onboarding and successful integration of contingent workers, maximizing operational efficiency.

- **Measuring Tips:** Set clear benchmarks for expected productivity levels at different time intervals post-hire and use performance tracking tools to gather data.

Innovation and Continuous Improvement Contributions

- **Metric Overview:** Quantify the number and impact of innovations or process improvements contributed by contingent workers.

- **Why It Matters:** Engaged workers are more likely to propose innovative ideas and improvements, fostering organizational growth and adaptability.

- **Measuring Tips:** Create a structured system for submitting and tracking improvement proposals, and assess their impact on efficiency, cost savings, or revenue generation.

Compliance and Incident Rates

- **Metric Overview:** Monitor the rate of compliance with organizational policies and the incidence of workplace issues among the contingent workforces.

- **Why It Matters:** Effective engagement and communication strategies lead to better compliance and lower incident rates, reducing legal and operational risks.

- **Measuring Tips:** Regularly review compliance reports and incident logs, benchmarking against industry standards to identify areas needing attention.

Client Satisfaction and Feedback

- **Metric Overview:** Collect feedback from internal and external clients on the performance and impact of projects involving contingent workers.

- **Why It Matters:** Positive client feedback affirms the contingent workforce's ability to meet and exceed project expectations, evidencing successful engagement.

- **Measuring Tips:** Utilize post-project surveys and in-depth interviews with stakeholders to gauge satisfaction levels, focusing on areas of strength and improvement.

There is no single answer to whether an MSP or an internal PMO is better for your organization; it depends on what suits your specific needs best. The MSP model gives you smooth processes, cost savings, and large talent pools, but it may also reduce your cultural fit and make you reliant on the provider. On the other hand, an internal PMO gives you more control, cultural alignment, and flexible processes, but it requires a lot of resources and may not have the same advantage in finding talent as the MSP. In the end, the choice depends on what you value more for your contingent workforce strategy — scalability and efficiency, or control and integration?

Chapter 7: Classifications of Contractors in the Contingent Workforce

As we explore the complex world of managing a contingent workforce, it's important to understand the different types of contractors that operate in this dynamic field. What's the reason for this? Well, firstly, not all heroes have capes, and likewise, not all contractors have the same profile. The contingent workforce is a diversity of talent, skills, and expertise, enabling organizations to find the ideal match for their changing needs.

Let's look at the main types of workers in this domain. First, we have the independent contractors, who work as freelancers without a regular employer to tie them down. Next, we have the consultants, who offer their expert advice on specific projects and often leave some valuable insights before they move on to their next assignment. And finally, we have temporary workers, who help with the tasks that employees cannot do due to absences, increased workload, or the lack of certain skills in-house.

Working in the contingent workforce is not just about meeting and working with different people and skills; it also involves dealing with complex legal and regulatory issues. This can seem like trying to crack a code without any clues. But knowing and following these legal rules is essential. Misclassifying a worker as an independent contractor? That's a sure way to get into legal trouble you want to avoid. Different classifications have different regulations on taxes, benefits, and rights, so it's important for organizations to be aware and compliant.

So, why does all this matter? Well, beyond the basic legal compliance, understanding the nuanced distinctions between contractor types enables organizations to better tailor their talent acquisition strategies. It's like having a Swiss Army knife at your disposal; each tool serves a unique purpose based on the task at hand. By effectively leveraging the diverse classifications within the contingent workforce, companies can foster a more agile, resilient, and competitive business model.

As we tip-toe through the tulips of contingent workforce management, let's embrace the diverse bouquet of contractor classifications. Recognizing and appreciating these differences not only helps in staying on the right side of the law but also unlocks the door to a world of strategic talent optimization. Remember, in the grand chess game of workforce planning, understanding the powers and movements of your pieces is key to a checkmate. So, let's keep our eyes on the board and play smart.

Types of Contractors and Their Classifications

The contingent workforce is a complex and dynamic environment, where different types of contractors have different needs and characteristics. This exploration seeks to understand how contractors can be categorized and distinguished, enabling talent consultants and contingent workforce managers to adjust their approaches accordingly.

Leading the charge are independent contractors. These individuals are the vanguards of the workforce, providing their services directly to businesses without the intermediation of an agency. Cherishing the autonomy their status affords, they have the liberty to select their projects and dictate their schedules. For organizations, leveraging independent contractors is a strategic maneuver, potentially reducing overhead expenses while bringing in specialized expertise on demand.

Another group that is most popular among MSPs are temporary staffing agency workers. These W2 workers come from the large talent pools of staffing agencies, and they offer organizations a mix of flexibility and convenience—helping them to easily adjust workforce size, speed up recruitment processes, and access a variety of skills for different needs. The main feature of staffing agency workers is that they are employed by the staffing agency, not the client company they are working for, even though they do work at the client's site or for the client's benefit. This relationship lets companies efficiently manage workforce size and costs without the long-term obligation or overhead of hiring permanent employees. Moreover, these workers can seamlessly join existing teams to keep up productivity levels during busy times or for specific projects, with the staffing agency taking care of all employment aspects, including HR and compliance duties.

Freelancers represent another pivotal group. Envision the creative virtuoso or the technological savant, offering their skills across the globe. Flourishing on project-based engagements, freelancers provide companies with a spectrum of creativity and innovation. Preferring the autonomy of self-employment, they are key players in the gig economy, offering a blend of flexibility and specialized knowledge.

We also encounter consultants, the oracles of the professional world. Armed with profound expertise in their respective fields, consultants are engaged to dissect issues and formulate strategies. Businesses frequently seek consultants for their deep insights and strategic guidance, leveraging their expertise to tackle complex challenges and drive transformation.

Lastly, temporary workers. These people fill roles, join teams smoothly for busy periods, project rollouts, or leave replacements, and then exit gracefully. Unlike workers from temporary staffing agencies, these contractors are hired by the company directly for short-term contracts without using a staffing agency. These workers may be hired for similar reasons as those from staffing agencies—such as high-demand seasons, special projects, or to cover for leaves of absence—but the hiring company handles the recruitment, onboarding, and payroll processes internally. Direct hiring allows companies to have more control over the selection and management of these workers but also requires them to deal with the complications of employment laws, worker compensation, and benefits administration on their own.

The classification further nuances itself when we dive into specialized niches, such as technology contractors known for their programming prowess or creative contractors who sprinkle their artistic magic on projects. Each niche fills a specific void, creating a mosaic of capabilities that businesses can leverage.

Understanding the legal classifications of these workers is also paramount. From W-2 employees vs. 1099-MISC independent contractors in the U.S., the distinction influences tax obligations, benefits, and compliance regulations. It's a treacherous terrain, rife with legal pitfalls for the unwary. As such, it's crucial for businesses and their contingent workforce managers to navigate these waters with the precision of a seasoned captain.

Let's imagine for a bit the growing trend of digital nomads. They are not an official category, but a reflection of how work is changing. These experts in technology have made the world their office, showing the adaptability and global reach of today's workforce.

Each type of contractor has its own benefits and drawbacks. Independent contractors, while having specialized skills, may need more supervision to be on the same page with project goals. Staffing agency workers have speed and flexibility, but they might take time to learn the company culture. Freelancers and consultants can offer creative solutions, but it might be hard to hire them when they are in high demand.

Temporary workers, while filling urgent staffing gaps, require attention to integration and continuity within teams. It becomes clear that smart contingent workforce leaders must manage a diverse team, ensuring the right balance of talent to meet business goals.

The classification of contractors extends beyond mere taxonomy—it's about understanding the pulse of the contingent workforce. It's about recognizing that behind each classification lies a palette of opportunities, challenges, and considerations that shape the strategic deployment of talent.

To succeed in this complicated industry, companies need to understand the types and traits of contractors very well. This helps them make smart choices, making sure that their strategy for using temporary workers is not only strong but also subtle and flexible.

As we've traversed the various classifications of contractors, it's clear that the contingent workforce is a tapestry of talent. Each thread, while distinct, contributes to the broader picture of agility, innovation, and strategic advantage. For talent consultants and contingent workforce leaders, mastering the art of contractor classifications is akin to possessing a key that unlocks immense potential.

To sum up, it is very important to be aware of the different kinds of contractors and their various categories. It helps businesses to move through the contingent workforce industry with assurance, making sure they can make the most of this varied pool of talent. So, as you plan your way through this dynamic environment, keep in mind that the key to your contingent workforce strategy is to know and value the diverse types of contractors available to you.

Legal and Regulatory Considerations

When addressing the classifications of contractors in the contingent workforce, it's crucial to navigate through a labyrinth of legal and regulatory considerations that not only vary by geography but also by the different types of employment relationships. To say that this can get as perplexing as trying to solve a Rubik's Cube in the dark is an understatement. But fear not, this section aims to illuminate the complexities in a manner that's digestible, if not slightly entertaining.

First, let's talk about the elephant in the room: misclassification. This can be as costly as accidentally buying a first-class ticket for your pet hamster. Misclassification occurs when an employee is incorrectly designated as an independent contractor or vice versa. This might not sound like a party foul, but the consequences can include hefty fines, back taxes, and legal complications. And let's be honest, no one wants the IRS crashing their party.

The legal landscape for contractors is also akin to shifting sands, with laws and regulations evolving to keep pace with the gig economy. For instance, the "ABC test" implemented in several states makes it tougher for businesses to classify workers as independent contractors. This test essentially says, if you want to classify someone as an independent contractor, they better be as independent as a teenager asserting their autonomy—otherwise, they're considered an employee.

But it's not all doom and gloom. With the proper know-how and due diligence, navigating the legalities can be as rewarding as finding an extra fry in your takeaway bag. For instance, knowing the difference between an independent contractor and an employee boils down to factors such as autonomy, contractual terms, and the nature of the work performed.

Contractual agreements are your best friend here. They're like the secret sauce to any successful contingent workforce program, specifying terms, conditions, and expectations for both parties. Think of them as the rulebook for your favorite board game—without it, things can get chaotic real quick.

Then we have the regulatory bodies to consider. Depending on your location and industry, you might be dealing with acronyms like the DOL (Department of Labor), IRS (Internal Revenue Service), or even OSHA (Occupational Safety and Health Administration). Each of these entities can have a say in how contractors should be treated, adding layers to our legal onion.

But wait, there's more. Internationally, the picture gets even more complex. For companies operating globally, compliance with local labor laws, such as GDPR in Europe for data protection or IR35 in the UK affecting off-payroll working, can feel like navigating a minefield with a blindfold. The key is to have a localized approach, understanding that what works in one country may not fly in another.

Intellectual property (IP) rights also enter the fray when dealing with contractors. In the battle for innovation, ensuring that your IP agreements are as tight as a drum is essential. Unlike traditional employee arrangements, IP generated by contractors doesn't automatically belong to the company unless explicitly stated. Yes, it's as important as remembering to wear pants to an in-person meeting.

And let's not forget about the data protection laws. With remote work becoming more common, understanding your obligations concerning personal data is crucial. It's not just about being a good corporate citizen; it's about not being on the receiving end of a data breach lawsuit, which can be as pleasant as a root canal but without the anesthesia.

Now, onto the penalties for non-compliance, which can range from monetary fines to reputational damage. It's like playing a game of Monopoly, but instead of just losing money, you might also lose your reputation and the trust of your stakeholders. Not exactly the kind of game night anyone hopes for.

Insurance requirements present another piece of the puzzle. Just as you wouldn't drive a car without insurance, employing or contracting with a workforce carries inherent risks that need to be mitigated. Worker's compensation, liability insurance, and professional indemnity insurance are just a few of the policies that can help protect against potential claims.

But there's light at the end of the tunnel. With careful planning, ongoing education, and the right tools, staying compliant doesn't have to feel like herding cats. Tools like Vendor Management Systems (VMS) and collaborations with knowledgeable legal partners can streamline compliance processes, keeping your contingent workforce program on the straight and narrow.

Lastly, it's essential to keep abreast of the latest developments in labor laws and workforce trends. Think of it as keeping your hand on the pulse of the gig economy—you wouldn't want to miss out on the next big thing or, worse, be caught off guard by a new regulation.

While the legal and regulatory landscape of managing a contingent workforce can seem daunting, approaching it with the right mix of diligence, humor, and adaptability can turn potential headaches into opportunities for optimization and growth. So, as you navigate through this maze, remember that the goal isn't just to avoid pitfalls but to build a resilient, flexible, and compliant workforce strategy that drives your business forward.

Chapter 8: Effective Supplier Management Strategies

As we delve into the crux of supplier management strategies, let's remember our ultimate quest for smooth sailing in managing our contingent workforce suppliers. It's akin to orchestrating a meticulously planned symphony, where each supplier plays a vital role in the opus of your business's success. At the heart of this, building and nurturing strong relationships with suppliers isn't just a good-to-have; it's an essential strategy for any organization keen on leveraging the full potential of its contingent workforce.

Why, you might ask, does this relationship saga between companies and their suppliers matter? In a sea of ever-evolving business landscapes, where agility and adaptability dictate the survival of the fittest, fostering a solid partnership with your suppliers ensures a mutual commitment to your business goals. It's about breaking the ice beyond formal contract negotiations to developing a rapport that stands the test of business upheavals. After all, when the chips are down, you'll want suppliers who'll stick with you through thick and thin, not those who'll ghost you at the first sight of trouble.

Onto the gripping chapter of evaluating and optimizing supplier performance, it's about unveiling the masked performance of your suppliers. Think of it as the unmasking ceremony at a masquerade. It's not enough to assume suppliers are delivering their A-game based on surface-level interactions. Regular performance reviews, constructive feedback loops, and transparent communication channels open the floor for continuous improvement. It propels suppliers from just being vendors to becoming invaluable partners who are as invested in your success as their own.

But wait, there's more to supplier management than heart-to-hearts and performance report cards. It's about strategizing for the long haul, envisioning a partnership that evolves and adapts over time. This entails aligning suppliers' strengths with your business objectives, seeking innovative solutions together, and leveraging their expertise to gain competitive advantages. It's the classic case of 1+1 equals 3, where the collaborative synergy between your organization and its suppliers unleashes potential you never knew existed.

As we wrap up this chapter, remember that effective supplier management strategies are more than just policies and procedures. They're about cultivating relationships, fine-tuning performance, and, most importantly, embracing suppliers as an extension of your business. As you march forward, arm yourselves with these strategies, and watch as your contingent workforce program flourishes into a formidable force, ready to tackle the dynamic challenges of the business world.

Building and Maintaining Strong Supplier Relationships

In the grand ballet of contingent workforce management, where every leap and pirouette must be executed with precision, building and maintaining strong supplier relationships is akin to mastering the art of a perfectly timed dance move. It's about more than just making sure your partners can keep pace; it's about creating a performance so synchronized, it elevates the entire production. Let's waltz through the essentials of how to orchestrate this harmony.

First thing's first: communication, the universal solvent for nearly every relationship, professional or otherwise. Clear, consistent, and candid communication creates a foundation of trust and understanding. It's not simply about relaying your needs and expectations to suppliers but also being open to their feedback and perspectives. This two-way street allows for adjustments and improvements, ensuring both parties are moving towards mutual goals in lockstep.

Understanding each supplier's capabilities and constraints is another pivotal step. Imagine you're about to embark on a wilderness adventure. Wouldn't you want to know the strengths and limitations of your guide? Similarly, in the contingent workforce landscape, appreciating what your suppliers can realistically achieve enables you to set achievable objectives, reducing friction and fostering a positive working relationship.

Partnerships flourish under the warm glow of mutual respect and recognition. Celebrating successes and milestones with your suppliers isn't just good manners; it's strategic. Acknowledging their contributions reinforces their value to your organization and encourages continued excellence and innovation. Remember, a little appreciation goes a long way in cementing a strong and enduring partnership.

Now, let's talk about flexibility. In an era where change is the only constant, the ability to adapt swiftly and smoothly is invaluable. Flexibility in dealing with your suppliers—whether it's regarding contract terms, project timelines, or last-minute changes—demonstrates that you're a partner who's willing to work through challenges together, rather than a rigid taskmaster. This flexibility makes your company a preferred client to do business with, ensuring long-term commitment from your suppliers.

Commitment to joint problem-solving is the glue that holds strong supplier relationships together. Challenges and setbacks are inevitable, but the focus should always be on finding solutions rather than assigning blame. Approaching problems with a collaborative mindset fosters innovation and can turn potential crises into opportunities for strengthening the partnership.

Transparency about future business needs and strategies can also serve to align suppliers more closely with your company's goals. When suppliers understand where your business is headed, they can proactively anticipate and cater to your evolving needs, leading to a more seamless and effective collaboration.

Nurturing supplier relationships also means investing in their growth and development. Whether by providing training, sharing industry insights, or involving them in strategic planning sessions, helping your suppliers improve their service offerings ultimately benefits your organization with enhanced capabilities and innovations.

Effective supplier relationship management entails regular performance evaluations, undertaken with a constructive and supportive approach. These assessments should not be perceived as a fault-finding mission but an opportunity for mutual growth and improvement. By setting clear metrics and benchmarks, both parties can objectively measure progress and identify areas for enhancement.

Lastly, remember that strong relationships are built on integrity. Honesty in your dealings, whether it pertains to meeting contractual obligations, timely payments, or publicly acknowledging your suppliers' contributions, cements your reputation as a trustworthy and reliable partner.

In summary, the art of building and maintaining strong supplier relationships in the contingent workforce realm is nuanced and multifaceted. It's about weaving a tapestry of trust, communication, flexibility, and mutual support. It involves celebrating successes and navigating challenges with grace. Above all, it's about recognizing that these relationships are not just transactional engagements but strategic partnerships that can propel your business to new heights.

As the curtain falls on this section, may you step into the spotlight with confidence, knowing that mastering the dance of supplier relationships is well within your grasp. And as you do, remember that it's the strength of these partnerships that will ultimately determine the success of your contingent workforce strategy, making every effort in this direction not just worthwhile, but essential.

Keeping these principles in mind, let's move forward, poised to foster relationships that not just endure but thrive, setting the stage for a future where your contingent workforce program is applauded for its outstanding performance, thanks in no small part to the symphony of strong supplier partnerships.

Evaluating and Optimizing Supplier Performance

Now, as we pivot from the foundational blocks and delve into the nitty-gritty of supplier management, there's an elephant in the room that we can't ignore. The cornerstone of any fruitful relationship with your suppliers rests on robust evaluation and optimization strategies. Think of it as keeping the engine of your car running smoothly; neglect it, and you might just find yourself stranded on the highway of inefficiencies and missed opportunities.

At heart, evaluating supplier performance isn't about pointing fingers or mounting a high horse. It's an exercise in alignment, ensuring that the cogs of your supplier machinery are well-oiled and turning in harmony with your business objectives. The first step, unsurprisingly, is setting clear, measurable KPIs. Think delivery times, quality standards, cost management, and innovation contributions as starting points. These aren't just arbitrary thresholds. They are the signposts guiding your supplier journey.

Setting KPIs is one step; accurately measuring them is another. This is where many organizations find themselves struggling amidst a deluge of data. The solution? Adopting a balanced scorecard methodology. It transcends mere quantitative analysis to include qualitative feedback from various stakeholders across the organization. After all, metrics can quantify speed, but they don't necessarily indicate direction.

So, what's next with this wealth of information? Suppose your analysis reveals your supplier's performance is inconsistent. It's crucial then to not just observe but to engage. Performance evaluation must be dialogic, involving a shared review of data and collaborative identification of improvement areas. This process is not solely about remediation but is a conduit for innovation and added value, extending beyond contractual obligations.

This means contracts should be viewed as living documents, not set-and-forget agreements. Regular evaluations of performance can reveal chances for renegotiation, enabling changes that match both the current business needs and market trends. The goal is to create a contract that is as flexible and adaptable as the market environment itself.

Technology can play a pivotal role in this symphony of supplier management. A robust Vendor Management System (VMS) isn't just a tool for tracking performance; it's your GPS for navigating the supplier mentality. It can help automate the mundane, freeing up your team to focus on strategic analysis and supplier development efforts.

Now, let's talk about the elephant in the room - underperformance. Despite your best efforts, sometimes things just don't click. Before you consider cutting ties, explore performance improvement plans. These should be collaborative efforts, with clear milestones and support mechanisms. Think of it as a relationship intervention, where both parties are committed to making it work.

In the spirit of continuous improvement, don't overlook the potential of supplier development programs. Investing in your suppliers' capabilities can yield significant returns, from innovation to improved sustainability practices. It's a win-win strategy that strengthens your supplier ecosystem.

However, it's essential to remember that optimizing supplier performance isn't a one-time project; it's an ongoing journey. The market dynamics, your business strategy, and technologies are continually evolving. Your supplier evaluation and optimization strategies should be agile, adapting to these changes to harness new opportunities and navigate challenges.

In the collaborative dance of supplier management, transparency is key. Open lines of communication foster trust and partnership. Regularly scheduled check-ins, joint strategizing sessions, and shared dashboards can provide the visibility needed to keep both parties aligned and focused on mutual success.

Risk management is another critical component. By integrating risk assessment into your evaluation process, you can proactively identify and mitigate potential disruptions before they impact your business. This forward-thinking approach can safeguard your supply chain and maintain business continuity.

So, as we wrap up this chapter, remember that evaluating and optimizing supplier performance is not about keeping score. It's about maximizing value for both parties, fostering innovation, and ensuring your suppliers are not just vendors but strategic partners in your success. Embrace the journey, be ready to adapt, and always keep the lines of communication open. After all, in the dynamic world of supplier management, the only constant is change.

Remember, the heart of effective supplier management beats to the rhythm of collaboration, innovation, and mutual growth. By adopting a holistic approach to evaluating and optimizing supplier performance, organizations can navigate the complexities of the contingent workforce industry and drive sustainable, long-term success.

Chapter 9: Artificial Intelligence in Contingent Workforce

As we pivot from the meticulous process of managing supplier relationships detailed in the previous chapter, we land squarely in the realm where technology and human resources intersect with remarkable impact: the utilization of Artificial Intelligence (AI) within the contingent workforce. While AI has the potential to transform contingent workforce management, it's important to remember that it should only be implemented when it addresses specific challenges that cannot be effectively managed by existing processes. Organizations must first evaluate their current workforce management systems and identify clear pain points such as slow hiring times, compliance risks, or difficulty handling large volumes of talent. If these challenges persist despite other improvements, AI might provide the solution.

Before diving into AI implementation, it's critical to conduct a feasibility audit to ensure that your systems can support AI integration, and that your data is clean, comprehensive, and consistent enough for AI to work effectively. AI should enhance decision-making and operational efficiency, not complicate processes that are already functioning well. Additionally, AI is most valuable when there is sufficient data to generate meaningful insights—without reliable data, AI's effectiveness diminishes rapidly.

The narrative of AI in this sector isn't just about futuristic toolkits or cold automation processes; it's a lively dance of innovation that's reshaping the way talent consultants and contingent workforce leaders approach talent acquisition and management. Through a veil of algorithms and data analytics, AI emerges as the unsung hero, capable of streamlining operations and magnifying the human effort.

Algorithms now have the power to sift through vast amounts of data to match skills with needs more accurately than ever before. This doesn't only speed up the hiring process but ensures a better fit between contractors and projects, reducing turnover and boosting project success rates. Artificial Intelligence is transforming decision-making processes within contingent workforce management. AI-powered tools, such as Applicant Tracking Systems (ATS), leverage semantic search algorithms to match candidates with job roles by understanding the context and nuances of job descriptions and resumes. This method goes beyond simple keyword matching and ensures a more profound alignment between candidate qualifications and job requirements. With AI, decision-making is no longer based on intuition alone but is supported by data, reducing biases and improving workforce outcomes. By integrating AI into contingent workforce strategies, organizations can automate time-consuming tasks like resume screening and onboarding. For example, AI-powered Applicant Tracking Systems (ATS) can scan thousands of resumes, rank candidates based on qualifications, and schedule interviews automatically. This not only speeds up the hiring process but also reduces administrative overhead. Similarly, AI can streamline onboarding by automating tasks such as contract generation, compliance checks, and training module assignments, freeing HR professionals to focus on more strategic activities. Furthermore, AI's predictive analytics tools are revolutionizing talent management by forecasting project outcomes, worker engagement levels, and even potential compliance issues before they arise. This proactive approach to management is akin to having a crystal ball, allowing leaders to navigate the contingent workforce landscape with unprecedented precision. Another vital function of AI is its ability to perform predictive analytics. By analyzing trends in workforce performance and engagement, AI can forecast future needs and identify potential issues before they arise. For instance, predictive analytics can be used to gauge project success rates, anticipate compliance challenges, and flag potential talent shortages, enabling organizations to respond proactively rather than reactively. AI is particularly adept at managing workforce disruptions by offering real-time insights and predictive capabilities. When sudden disruptions occur—such as shifts in project demands, unexpected employee turnover, or external market changes—AI systems can swiftly analyze the impact and suggest optimized solutions. For example, AI can predict skill gaps that may arise from disruptions and automatically recommend contingency plans, such as reallocating talent from other projects or initiating rapid recruitment drives for temporary workers.

Additionally, AI can track workforce performance in real time, identifying early warning signs of disengagement, burnout, or compliance risks. By proactively flagging these issues, AI enables workforce leaders to intervene before small disruptions escalate into major operational problems. This ability to respond dynamically helps organizations maintain agility, ensuring that disruptions are managed efficiently and with minimal impact on overall performance.

Yet, what truly sets AI apart in this field isn't its computational prowess alone. It's the marriage of technology with human intuition that creates a synergy, fostering a more nuanced approach to decision making and efficiency. AI enhances predictive analytics by learning from historical data patterns and identifying trends that might not be immediately visible to human analysts. Through machine learning algorithms, AI systems can detect anomalies and predict outcomes with higher accuracy, offering early warnings on workforce challenges like potential talent shortages, compliance risks, or team productivity dips. This advanced foresight allows workforce leaders to take proactive measures, adjust hiring strategies, and allocate resources more efficiently, ensuring that their contingent workforce remains resilient and adaptable to future demands. For instance, when leveraged for performance evaluations, AI can provide quantifiable insights that, when combined with managerial intuition, pave the way for more informed and balanced assessments. A key advantage of AI in recruitment is its potential to reduce unconscious bias. Algorithms evaluate candidates based on objective criteria like skills and experience, helping to level the playing field. However, it's crucial to ensure that AI tools are regularly audited to avoid perpetuating existing biases through flawed data inputs. Periodic algorithm reviews and integrating transparent decision-making frameworks will enhance the fairness of AI systems, aligning them with organizational diversity goals and reducing compliance risks. This harmonious alliance between AI and human judgment empowers program consultants and contingent workforce leaders to sculpt strategies that are not just data-driven, but also deeply resonant with the individual nuances of their workforce.

Perhaps the most compelling aspect of integrating AI into the contingent workforce arena is its potential to democratize opportunities. By eliminating unconscious bias and standardizing the initial screening processes, AI levels the playing field, ensuring that candidates are evaluated based on their skills and potential rather than extraneous factors. This shift towards a more inclusive and equitable hiring practice not only enhances the reputation of companies but also enriches the overall talent pool, driving innovation and productivity.

As we venture deeper into this technological odyssey, it becomes evident that AI is not here to replace the human element but to augment it, to recalibrate our approach towards talent acquisition and management in the contingent workforce sector. The blend of AI's analytical might with human insight offers a beacon of efficiency and innovation, guiding talent consultants and contingent workforce leaders towards more strategic, fair, and impactful decision-making processes. Despite its advantages, integrating AI into contingent workforce management can significantly disrupt established workflows if not implemented thoughtfully. AI tools often require changes in daily operations, such as shifting from manual decision-making processes to automated systems. This transition can create friction among team members who may be unfamiliar or uncomfortable with AI technologies. Additionally, AI's reliance on data requires businesses to restructure their data collection and analysis workflows, which can initially slow down operations as teams adjust to new procedures.

These disruptions may lead to temporary reductions in productivity as employees learn how to work with AI-driven platforms. For instance, the shift from traditional candidate screening methods to AI-powered recruitment processes might demand retraining HR teams on how to interpret AI-generated insights. Organizations must also be cautious of AI's potential to introduce new challenges, such as decision-making opacity— where employees may not fully understand how AI arrived at a particular recommendation. To mitigate these risks, it's essential to provide sufficient training, foster a culture of adaptability, and ensure transparency in how AI systems function within the workforce.

As we look towards the future, it's clear that AI will continue to play a pivotal role in shaping the dynamics of the contingent workforce, ensuring that the field remains adaptable, resilient, and, above all, human.

The Role of AI in Talent Acquisition and Management

After looking at the wider impact of Artificial Intelligence on the contingent workforce industry, let's focus on a very interesting topic: AI's role in finding and managing talent. Now, don't assume this section is going to be boring: it's more exciting than getting a bonus chicken nugget in your fast-food order.

First things first, AI is redefining the playbook for sourcing top-tier talent. Imagine a world where resumes are screened not by the weary eyes of HR professionals but by algorithms sharp enough to slice through the fluff and pinpoint the crème de la crème. This is no pipe dream. AI-driven applications are increasingly taking the lead in scanning literally thousands of profiles to identify candidates whose experience, skills, and potential align perfectly with a company's needs. It's like having a superhero recruiter on your team - minus the cape.

But AI's magic doesn't end at recruitment; it extends its golden touch to talent management too. Picture software so intuitive, it not only tracks an employee's performance but also predicts their career trajectory within the company. This crystal-ball-esque capability enables organizations to design personalized growth plans for every individual, ensuring that both the employee's and the company's futures are as bright as a supernova.

Let's talk about candidate engagement. In the romance of recruitment, AI plays the role of Cupid, automating communication in a way that keeps prospects engaged and informed without the process feeling as impersonal as a robocall. Whether it's scheduling interviews or providing timely updates, AI ensures that the candidate experience is as smooth as the jazz playing in an elevator.

Onboarding is another stage where AI brings its A-game. Gone are the days of drowning in paperwork on your first day. AI-driven onboarding platforms are like digital butlers, guiding new hires through necessary procedures, paperwork, and training sessions with an efficiency that would put Jeeves to shame.

Performance management, too, has seen a revolution courtesy of AI. By analyzing data on work patterns, productivity levels, and even team dynamics, AI tools can provide insights that are as revealing as seeing your work habits under a microscope. It's all in the name of helping managers and teams optimize performance and foster a culture of continuous improvement.

Let's not overlook the role of AI in learning and development. Tailored learning paths? Check. Identification of skill gaps? Double-check. AI in this realm is like a wise mentor, offering resources and learning opportunities that are not just relevant but also timely, ensuring that the workforce remains agile and up-to-date. It's professional development with a turbocharger.

Then there's the realm of employee engagement. Imagine software that can measure morale and engagement levels in real-time, providing insights that can help nip potential issues in the bud before they blossom into full-blown problems. It's like having a mood ring for your organization, but considerably more accurate.

And let's not forget about the data. Oh, the glorious data. AI thrives on it, and talent acquisition and management are no exceptions. By analyzing trends, patterns, and outliers, AI can help predict future staffing needs, flag potential retention issues, and even recommend strategies for maintaining a happy, motivated workforce. It's like having a crystal ball, but one grounded in data rather than mysticism.

However, integrating AI into talent acquisition and management is not without its challenges. There's the issue of data privacy, the need for transparency in how AI makes decisions, and of course, the perpetual dance of keeping the human in human resources. It's a tightrope walk, but one that can lead to a veritable utopia of efficiency and engagement when done right.

The role of AI in talent acquisition and management is something akin to a revolution; a bold reimagining of traditional processes, supercharged with efficiency, personalization, and insights that were once the stuff of science fiction. As we navigate this brave new world, it's essential to approach it with a blend of enthusiasm and caution, embracing the opportunities while mindfully navigating the challenges.

So, as we march forward into this exciting future, let's keep our wits about us and our eyes on the prize. The fusion of AI and human ingenuity in managing talent is not just a trend; it's the next frontier. And trust me, it's one heck of a ride.

In the grand tapestry of contingent workforce management, AI's role in talent acquisition and management is a vibrant thread, weaving together the future of work with precision, insight, and a touch of humor. After all, in a world where robots are our coworkers, a little bit of laughter goes a long way. So, let's embrace this journey with open arms and a can-do attitude, prepared to tackle whatever challenges and opportunities come our way.

Leveraging AI for Improved Decision Making and Efficiency

Artificial Intelligence (AI) in contingent labor isn't just a buzzword or a distant tomorrow's dream. It's here, reshaping the very framework of how decisions are made, and efficiencies are unearthed. For talent consultants, program consultants, and those blazing trails in contingent workforce leadership, AI isn't the future; it is the indefatigable assistant they didn't know they needed.

AI thrives in complex environments where vast amounts of data are involved. It analyzes patterns and trends that would be difficult or impossible for humans to detect in a short timeframe. By doing so, AI helps leaders make more informed decisions based on data-driven insights rather than intuition alone. This ability to process and interpret large datasets allows AI to optimize workforce allocation, performance monitoring, and even resource planning. AI in Applicant Tracking Systems (ATS) brings a suite of advancements that directly address the evolving recruitment demands of today's businesses. These systems leverage semantic search algorithms, powered by Natural Language Processing (NLP), to enhance the matching of candidates with job openings, going beyond the limitations of keyword matching to understand the context and nuances of job descriptions and resumes. This level of automation not only improves efficiency but also ensures a deeper compatibility between candidates and job requirements.

Let's cut to the chase - decision making is no trivial matter in the contingent workforce realm. It's the difference between striking gold with the perfect talent fit and a miss that could cost dearly. AI steps into this high-stakes arena as a critical advantage. The AI-powered ATS tool has the potential to reduce hiring biases.

By objectively analyzing resumes and qualifications, these systems help prevent unconscious human biases from influencing the hiring process. In your role, leveraging AI can ensure fair and unbiased candidate evaluations, aligning perfectly with expertise in Talent Management and Vendor Management Systems. This objectivity is crucial in creating a more diverse and inclusive workforce.

However, the fairness of AI-powered ATS systems relies on regular audits to check for any inadvertent biases. As a Talent Management Expert, advising clients to conduct periodic reviews of their ATS algorithms is essential. This involves analyzing hiring data to identify patterns that could indicate bias, ensuring that the AI systems are indeed providing an equitable platform for all candidates. Systems integration with other HR software is also crucial, as it improves both internal and external communication, further streamlining the recruitment process.

The reliance on AI to automate recruitment processes marks a significant shift towards more efficient, unbiased, and effective talent acquisition strategies. However, it's essential to implement AI ethically by ensuring transparency in how decisions are made and auditing AI algorithms regularly to prevent unintentional biases. By maintaining ethical oversight, organizations can build trust with both candidates and internal teams, ensuring that AI-driven processes are fair and equitable. Yet, with great power comes great responsibility—the ethical deployment of AI in contingent workforce management underscores the importance of transparency, fairness, and accountability. These principles are fundamental in gaining trust and ensuring that decisions are made in the best interest of all stakeholders.

For those at the helm of contingent workforce strategies, the integration of AI isn't just a competitive advantage; it represents a pivotal shift towards a future where data-driven decisions, efficiency, and inclusivity are not aspirations but realities. This journey from data to decision, clutter to clarity, and potential to performance is a continuous cycle of learning and adaptation, powered by AI.

Embedding AI into the contingent workforce ecosystem augments human expertise, unlocking previously unseen trends and enabling leaders to pivot their strategies in real-time. This synergy between human intuition and AI's insights is where the future of contingent workforce management lies—a future that's already here, filled with opportunities waiting to be unlocked by the savvy, the curious, and the forward-thinking leaders ready to embark on this transformative journey.

As we delve deeper into the integration of AI with ATS, it's essential to highlight the ongoing evolution of these technologies. AI is not static; it continuously improves, learning from new data, user interactions, and feedback loops. This dynamic nature ensures that AI-powered ATS systems become more accurate and efficient over time, offering increasingly sophisticated insights into the recruitment process. For talent acquisition professionals, this means access to a tool that not only evolves with the market but also anticipates future trends and challenges. This capacity for predictive analysis is invaluable, enabling organizations to stay ahead in a competitive talent market by adapting their recruitment strategies in real-time.

Moreover, the role of AI in enhancing candidate experience cannot be overstated. In an era where the candidate journey is as critical as the outcome, AI-powered systems provide a more engaging and personalized interaction. From the initial job search to application and feedback, AI can tailor the process to meet the unique needs and preferences of each candidate. This personalized approach not only improves the candidate's experience but also boosts the employer's brand, attracting top talent by showcasing a commitment to innovation and inclusivity. By automating routine tasks, AI allows recruiters to focus on the human aspect of talent acquisition—building relationships, understanding candidate aspirations, and crafting compelling narratives that resonate with potential hires.

Finally, the strategic integration of AI within ATS systems signals a broader shift towards data-driven organizational cultures. In leveraging AI, companies are not just optimizing their recruitment processes; they're embedding a culture of innovation, continuous learning, and adaptability. This cultural shift is critical for thriving in the modern business, where agility and foresight are key to navigating uncertainties. AI's role extends beyond talent acquisition, influencing strategic decision-making across the organization. As companies become more adept at interpreting and acting on the insights provided by AI, they unlock new levels of efficiency, creativity, and competitive advantage. This holistic approach to AI integration underscores the transformative potential of technology—not just as a tool for operational excellence but as a catalyst for organizational evolution.

Welcome to the era of AI-driven contingent workforce management, where every decision is informed, every process is optimized, and every talent interaction is empowered.

Chapter 10: The Contingent Workforce Engagement Process

As we pivot from the cutting-edge advances of artificial intelligence in contingent workforce management, let's not forget the good ol' human element in the equation. The engagement process of the contingent workforce could best be described as a thrilling rollercoaster ride in the dark - you know there are ups, downs, and loop-the-loops coming, but exactly when is anybody's guess. The truth is, engaging a contingent workforce effectively requires a blend of strategy, analytics, and a dollop of good interpersonal skills. AI plays a crucial role in handling workforce disruptions, especially in volatile environments. By analyzing vast amounts of data, AI can predict potential risks, like project delays or labor shortages, before they occur. This proactive approach helps mitigate disruptions and ensures smoother workflows. AI can also reroute resources, suggest alternative workforce strategies, and dynamically adjust project timelines to maintain consistency even during turbulent periods.

Let's talk shop about best practices for effective engagement. It's like constructing a bridge. You need a solid foundation (clear understanding of needs), strong materials (the right contingent workers), and a competent builder (a stellar engagement strategy). Consider this; every interaction with your contingent workforce should enhance their connection to your organization, encourage high performance, and foster a synergistic relationship. From transparent communication about roles and expectations to offering support and resources necessary for their success, engagement is an art as much as it is science. Remember, they might not be with you forever, but while they are, they're as much a part of your team as your full-time employees.

Now, onto something that gets the analytical juices flowing - metrics for measuring the success of engagement strategies. You can't manage what you don't measure, right? From turnover rates and project completion time to quality of work and satisfaction levels, define what success looks like for your contingent workforce engagement. Perhaps it's the percentage of contingent workers who become brand ambassadors, or the innovation levels in projects they're involved in; whatever your KPIs, track them religiously. The data you'll gather is like breadcrumbs leading you through the forest to grandmother's house - it shows you where you're on track and where you might need to tweak your strategy.

Let's face it, engaging the contingent workforce is a little like speed dating. You have a short window to make a connection, figure out if your goals align, and decide if you want to "see each other again" on future projects. It asks for flexibility, quick thinking, and an ability to connect on both a professional and personal level. And just like dating, it's not just about finding the right match, but also about being the right match - presenting your organization as one where high-quality contingent workers want to contribute their skills and talents.

Engaging your contingent workforce effectively is about much more than just onboarding and managing projects. It's about building relationships, measuring what matters, and continuously improving your process. Do it right, and you might just find that your contingent workforce becomes one of your most valuable assets, driving innovation, flexibility, and success in this ever-changing world of work. Now, isn't that a ride worth taking?

Best Practices for Effective Engagement

So, we've already journeyed through the nuts and bolts of the contingent workforce engagement process. Now, let's zero in on the best practices for making your engagement not just effective, but spectacularly so. Imagine a world where every contingent worker feels like a part of the team, productivity skyrockets, and your organization's flexibility becomes its superpower. To turn that dream into reality, we've distilled wisdom from the field, sprinkled with a dash of humor and insight, into these guiding principles.

Communication is essential for our discussion. The main thing is to be transparent, but it's also a skill. Make sure that your contingent workers understand their responsibilities, but also encourage them to speak their minds and issues. It's like creating a two-way road where ideas can circulate easily, enhancing projects with varied perspectives.

Then there's integration. Contingent workers should feel as much a part of the team as full-time employees do. This means including them in relevant meetings, brainstorming sessions, and even the occasional after-work hangout. It's about creating a culture where everyone's on the same playing field, fostering a sense of belonging and collaboration.

On the theme of fairness, don't let your contingent workers feel like second-class citizens in the workplace. Offering them access to the same tools, resources, and perks as your permanent staff is a step towards breaking down barriers and building trust.

Training and development opportunities shouldn't be exclusive to your permanent staff. Investing in your contingent workers' growth shows that you value their contribution and are keen on their development within your organization. It's a win-win; they grow, and your projects benefit from their enhanced skills.

Feedback loops are essential. Regular check-ins not only help in aligning expectations but also provide a platform to recognize achievements and address concerns. Think of it as keeping your finger on the pulse, ensuring everyone's aligned and motivated.

Let's not forget about leveraging technology. Use digital tools and platforms to streamline communication, manage projects, and facilitate easier integration of contingent workers. It's like giving everyone a digital megaphone, only much less noisy and far more effective. While AI can be an incredibly powerful tool for optimizing contingent workforce processes, it should only be implemented when absolutely necessary. Deploying AI for the sake of technological advancement without a clear strategic need can lead to inefficiencies, resource wastage, and even worker disengagement. Before integrating AI into your engagement process, assess whether it adds tangible value to your operations, ensuring that it aligns with your organization's goals and workforce dynamics.

Vetting and onboarding processes are crucial too. A rigorous, yet swift vetting process ensures that you're bringing on board the right talent. And a smooth, informative onboarding experience can set the tone for a fruitful engagement right from the start.

Measuring the success of onboarding is essential to ensure that new contingent workers are set up for success and can quickly integrate into your workforce. Key metrics to track include:

- **Time-to-Productivity**: This metric measures how long it takes for a new contingent worker to reach full productivity. A shorter time-to-productivity indicates an effective onboarding process that equips workers with the necessary tools and knowledge to perform their role efficiently.

- **Completion Rates for Training Modules**: Tracking whether new workers complete mandatory training within the expected timeframe helps assess the clarity and effectiveness of the onboarding content.

- **Worker Feedback on Onboarding**: Gathering feedback from new contingent workers through surveys or interviews is a qualitative measure of onboarding success. Positive feedback typically indicates a smooth onboarding experience, while negative feedback can highlight areas for improvement.

- **Turnover During or Shortly After Onboarding**: A high turnover rate soon after onboarding could signal that the process is insufficient or that expectations were unclear. Reducing turnover in this critical phase is a strong indicator of success.

- **Compliance and Policy Adherence**: Ensuring that contingent workers are aware of and comply with organizational policies and procedures during onboarding is another vital metric. Monitoring compliance rates can identify gaps in onboarding effectiveness.

By closely monitoring these metrics, organizations can continuously refine their onboarding processes, ensuring that contingent workers are properly integrated and positioned for long-term success within the organization.

Understanding the legal environment is essential. By complying with labor laws and regulations, you safeguard your organization and demonstrate to your contingent workers that you respect their rights.

Cultivating a supportive environment is about more than just being friendly. It's about actively seeking to remove roadblocks to your contingent workers' success, providing them with the support they need to excel in their roles.

The importance of defining clear goals and roles can't be overstated. It equips your contingent workers with a clear roadmap, increasing their efficiency and effectiveness in contributing to your organization's objectives.

Flexibility goes both ways. Being open to adjusting project requirements or timelines based on feedback and evolving situations can lead to better outcomes and foster a culture of mutual respect.

Building a sense of community among your workforce, contingent or otherwise, can significantly enhance engagement and productivity. Initiatives like team-building activities or community forums can make everyone feel included and valued.

Encouraging innovation and initiative among your contingent workforce can unlock hidden potentials. When workers feel empowered to bring new ideas to the table, the results can often exceed expectations.

Finally, let's circle back to the importance of metrics. Regularly measure the effectiveness of your engagement strategies to identify what's working and where there's room for improvement. It's like having a roadmap that constantly updates itself, helping you steer clear of obstacles and towards success.

The secret sauce to effective engagement in the contingent workforce isn't so secret after all. It's a blend of communication, integration, fairness, and continuous improvement. By adhering to these principles, you're not just engaging workers; you're building a powerhouse of productivity and innovation. Here's to making every engagement a monumental success!

Metrics for Measuring Success of Engagement Strategies

Once we've got a solid grip on the best practices to engage our contingent workforce effectively, it's crucial to understand how we can tell if these strategies are hitting the mark. Without a doubt, the proof is in the pudding, or in our case, the metrics! Engagement isn't just a feel-good factor; it's a strategic asset that can be measured and optimized for better outcomes.

Retention rates are one of the classic metrics for measuring engagement success. High retention rates indicate that contingent workers are satisfied and willing to return for future projects. To measure retention, track the percentage of contingent workers who complete multiple projects or are rehired after initial engagements. A high rehiring rate is a strong indicator of engagement success.

Another important metric is time-to-productivity. This measures how quickly contingent workers reach optimal performance levels after onboarding. A shorter time-to-productivity suggests an efficient onboarding process and effective engagement. Use project milestones or predefined performance benchmarks to track how quickly new hires contribute to key deliverables.

Quality of work is also a critical metric, which can be measured through project outcomes, client satisfaction scores, and stakeholder feedback. High-quality work produced by contingent workers indicates effective engagement and alignment with project goals. Regular feedback sessions with internal teams and clients can help assess the quality of deliverables and uncover areas for improvement.

Engagement surveys are another useful tool. These can be deployed at key points during the contingent worker's tenure to gather data on satisfaction, alignment with goals, and the perceived level of support from the organization. Engagement scores over time help identify trends and areas for continuous improvement.

Turnover rates during a project or at the end of an engagement period can also reflect the effectiveness of your engagement strategy. A high turnover rate may indicate dissatisfaction or misalignment between the worker's expectations and the project's environment.

Finally, track innovation contributions. Engaged contingent workers are often more motivated to contribute new ideas. Keep a record of how many new processes, strategies, or solutions are suggested by contingent workers and assess their impact on the project or the organization.

AI-enhanced predictive analytics offer deeper insights into workforce trends by forecasting potential turnover, project delays, and even engagement levels. By processing data in real-time, AI can recommend actions such as altering project timelines, reassigning roles, or offering incentives to improve worker retention and productivity. This predictive ability ensures you stay ahead of potential workforce challenges before they become costly problems. High retention rates signify that workers are not only satisfied with their roles but are also aligned with your company's mission. This alignment creates a win-win scenario where contingent workers are eager to contribute their best work.

Next up is the metric of project completion rates. It's an often overlooked yet critical metric. A project running smoothly with minimal hiccups and reaching the finish line on time (or even ahead of time!) speaks volumes about the level of engagement and efficiency of your contingent workforce. Remember, a happy crew is a productive crew.

Then there's the quality of work metric. This goes beyond just getting the job done. We're talking about work that surpasses expectations and makes stakeholders sit up and take notice. This metric can be a bit subjective, but regular feedback sessions and quality assessments can provide a clear picture of performance standards being met or exceeded.

Another key metric to consider is the innovation and initiative level exhibited by contingent workers. Engaged workers are more likely to think outside the box and bring fresh ideas to the table. Tracking the number of new ideas implemented or the instances where contingent workers go above and beyond can shed light on engagement levels.

Don't overlook the importance of feedback, both given and received. High rates of constructive feedback demonstrate an open communication channel, which is crucial for engagement. It indicates that contingent workers feel valued and part of the team, enough to contribute their insights for mutual improvement.

Let's not forget about the Net Promoter Score (NPS). While typically used to gauge customer satisfaction, it can be repurposed to understand contingent worker satisfaction. A high NPS indicates that your contingent workforce would recommend your company as a great place to work, underscoring successful engagement.

Time-to-productivity is another metric that can't be ignored. How quickly does a contingent worker get up to speed and start contributing effectively? A short ramp-up time suggests that your onboarding process is efficient, and workers feel equipped and motivated to dive into their roles.

Engagement surveys can also provide a goldmine of data. Regularly conducted, these surveys can track how engagement levels change over time and pinpoint areas of improvement. They offer direct insight into the contingent workforce's perceptions and experiences.

Employee referral rates among your contingent workforce are another telling metric. High referral rates imply strong engagement levels as satisfied and engaged contingent workers are more likely to refer peers to join your company.

Utilization rates are crucial too. They help you understand if the skills of your contingent workforce are being utilized to their fullest potential. High utilization rates indicate that workers are engaged in meaningful work that matches their skill set.

Performance against objectives is a straightforward metric. Setting clear goals and measuring contingent workers' performance against these goals can provide clear insights into their engagement and productivity levels.

Attendance and punctuality records can also offer engagement clues. Although contingent roles can often be remote or flexible, patterns of late submissions or absences might indicate disengagement, while consistent punctuality and attendance suggest high levels of commitment.

In an era where digital platforms reign supreme, engagement can also be measured through digital interactions. Analyzing engagement levels on project management tools, communication platforms, and other digital workspaces can offer a modern twist on gauging engagement levels.

Finally, let's talk about cultural alignment—a bit nebulous but incredibly important. A contingent workforce that feels aligned with your company's values and culture is more likely to be engaged and productive. This can be measured through direct questions in engagement surveys that probe into the cultural fit.

Measuring the success of engagement strategies for your contingent workforce isn't just about crunching numbers. It's about understanding the human element and creating an environment where people are motivated to bring their best selves to work. By keeping a keen eye on these metrics, you can ensure that your contingent workforce is not just engaged but fully integrated into the fabric of your organization.

And let's face it, that's when the magic happens.

Industry-Specific Contingent Workforce Strategies

The demand for qualified professionals often outpaces supply. Strategic approaches to workforce management are not just beneficial—they are essential. The healthcare industry is a prime example where contingent workforce strategies have become essential due to chronic staffing shortages. For instance, the

University of Pittsburgh Medical Center (UPMC) implemented a contingent workforce strategy to manage staffing levels across its hospitals. By hiring temporary nurses, doctors, and other healthcare professionals during peak times, UPMC has been able to meet patient care demands without compromising service quality. This contingent strategy is supported by a rigorous vetting process and workforce management platforms that ensure compliance with healthcare regulations and maintain high standards of patient care.

In the **manufacturing industry**, contingent workforce strategies are often employed to respond to fluctuating production cycles and market demand. Companies like Baxter, a global medical device manufacturer, utilize managed service programs (MSP) to harmonize workforce management across locations. By using contingent labor, they can adjust their staffing levels based on production needs, reducing costs associated with permanent staffing during slower periods. This strategy allows Baxter to stay competitive while maintaining flexibility and meeting regulatory standards.

The **technology sector** is another key adopter of contingent workforce strategies. Companies like IBM and Microsoft regularly employ highly specialized contingent workers to manage short-term projects that require niche expertise, such as AI development or cybersecurity. By tapping into a global talent pool, these companies ensure they can meet project deadlines and innovate without being constrained by a permanent workforce. Additionally, the use of Vendor Management Systems (VMS) allows these companies to manage talent across different time zones and regions while ensuring compliance with local labor laws.

Each of these industries demonstrates how a tailored contingent workforce strategy can provide operational flexibility, cost savings, and access to specialized talent. However, the **key to success** lies in understanding the specific challenges of the industry—whether it's healthcare's strict regulatory environment, manufacturing's fluctuating demand cycles, or technology's need for rapid innovation—and designing a strategy that aligns with these unique needs.

One such example is the University of Pittsburgh Medical Center (UPMC) implementing a contingent workforce strategy to manage the staffing at its hospitals. UPMC's strategy included hiring temporary nurses and other healthcare professionals to fill the gaps in their staffing.

To design an effective program structure for a healthcare contingent workforce strategy, it is important to understand the organization's needs, goals, and challenges. UPMC's approach to contingent workforce management is multifaceted, emphasizing not only the immediate need for staffing but also the long-term implications for patient care and organizational efficiency. By integrating temporary nurses and healthcare professionals into their staffing model, UPMC has been able to maintain high levels of service and care even during periods of significant staffing demand fluctuations. This strategy highlights the critical role that contingent labor can play in ensuring that healthcare providers can meet patient needs without compromise.

The decision to employ contingent labor, particularly in healthcare, is accompanied by a rigorous vetting process to ensure that all temporary staff meet UPMC's high standards for care and professionalism. This includes comprehensive background checks, verification of credentials, and a structured orientation process to integrate contingent staff seamlessly into the existing team. Such measures are crucial in maintaining the quality of care and upholding the trust that patients place in their healthcare institutions.

Moreover, UPMC's strategic use of contingent labor is supported by robust workforce management systems that enable effective scheduling, tracking, and communication across the organization. These systems ensure that the deployment of temporary staff is both efficient and effective, addressing gaps in staffing without disrupting the continuity of care.

This case study not only underscores the importance of contingent labor in the healthcare industry but also serves as a blueprint for other organizations facing similar challenges. By adopting a strategic and systematic approach to contingent workforce management, healthcare providers can enhance their flexibility, responsiveness, and overall capacity to deliver exceptional care.

A global medical device company, Baxter, shows how using a contingent workforce can help deal with the challenges of production cycles and market demands in manufacturing. By implementing a managed service program (MSP), Baxter sought to harmonize its workforce management across multiple locations, addressing the inefficiencies inherent in a decentralized staffing supplier network.

The company's objectives were clear and ambitious: to establish a scalable and quality-driven contingent workforce program that ensures continuity, value, and wage parity. The introduction of vendor management and workforce planning technology solutions was pivotal in achieving these goals, allowing for enhanced tracking, management, and analysis of the contingent workforce throughout the enterprise. This strategic move was not just about filling gaps in staffing; it was about elevating the entire recruitment process to meet headcount requirements effectively and improve recruitment efforts.

Action was taken swiftly and thoughtfully. The implementation plans included:

1. Gathering contingent worker data for cost analysis

2. Establishing service level metrics

3. Integrating technology solutions for comprehensive workforce management

This approach ensured minimal disruption to the company's core operations, allowing for a smooth transition to the new model.

The results speak volumes about the efficacy of a well-orchestrated contingent workforce strategy. The company witnessed significant cost reductions, process improvements, and higher levels of contractor retention. Moreover, the administrative burden was alleviated, compliance and co-employment risks were minimized, and data integrity was enhanced through the integration of centralized platforms.

This case study exemplifies the transformative power of contingent workforce strategies in the manufacturing sector. It illustrates how strategic planning, technology integration, and a focus on quality and efficiency can lead to substantial operational improvements with the additional benefit of cost savings. For companies in the manufacturing industry, embracing a contingent workforce strategy can be a game-changer in achieving business agility and sustained growth.

The technology industry, characterized by rapid innovation and fluctuating project demands, increasingly relies on contingent workforce strategies to access specialized skills, and manage workforce flexibility. Companies like IBM have leveraged contingent labor to fill gaps in staffing for technology projects. This ensures that they have the right talent for specific tasks without the long-term commitment of traditional employment. This approach allows for adaptability in a competitive market, where the demand for niche digital skills can outpace the supply of available workers. By utilizing contingent labor, technology firms can quickly scale their workforce up or down based on project needs while simultaneously optimizing productivity, and reducing costs associated with under or overstaffing. This strategic use of contingent labor is instrumental in maintaining a competitive edge in the fast-paced tech industry.

The integration of contingent labor within the technology sector not only addresses immediate project needs but also fosters an environment of innovation and agility. Firms like Google, IBM, and Microsoft have demonstrated the effectiveness of this strategy by engaging highly specialized contingent workers for complex, time-sensitive projects. This approach allows technology companies to remain at the forefront of industry advancements without the overhead of maintaining a large, permanent staff.

Moreover, the strategic use of contingent labor empowers technology companies to explore new markets and technologies with reduced risk. By employing experts on a project basis, these companies can pilot new initiatives and rapidly scale operations in response to successful outcomes. This flexibility is crucial in an industry defined by constant change and competition.

The adoption of advanced workforce management platforms further enhances the value of contingent labor in the technology sector. These platforms provide real-time insights into workforce composition, performance, and costs, enabling more informed decision-making and efficient resource allocation. The data-driven nature of these systems aligns well with the tech industry's emphasis on analytics and optimization.

Additionally, the emphasis on diversity and innovation within the technology sector is supported by a contingent workforce strategy. By drawing from a broader pool of global talent, technology companies can introduce fresh perspectives and skills that drive creative solutions and market differentiation. This diversity of thought is critical for innovation and adapting to global market demands.

All industries embracing contingent workforce strategies exemplify a forward-thinking approach to talent management. By using the adaptability, expertise, and creativity of contingent workers, companies can overcome the difficulties of a changing industry environment, thereby securing their ongoing development and success.

Chapter 11: Future Trends in Contingent Workforce Management

As we've journeyed through contingent workforce management, we've unpacked the nuts and bolts, flirted with the complexities, and navigated through the maze of best practices. Now, as we stand on the precipice of what's next, it's about time we delve into the crystal ball of contingent workforce management. The future is as exciting as it is unpredictable, jam-packed with technological innovations and evolving workforce dynamics that promise to shake up the status quo. Let's dive into what's on the horizon and how preparing for these shifts can turn challenges into opportunities.

First up, the digital transformation is not just knocking on our door; it's bulldozing through walls. The adoption of sophisticated technologies like artificial intelligence (AI), machine learning, and blockchain is not merely a fleeting trend but the bedrock upon which the future of contingent workforce management will be built. These technologies are poised to revolutionize how we source, manage, and engage with contingent talent. Imagine an AI-driven platform that can predict staffing needs based on market trends or blockchain technology that ensures the authenticity of a contractor's credentials. The possibilities are only limited by our willingness to embrace change.

With the digital revolution in full swing, the contingent workforce is also evolving. The gig economy is morphing into something more nuanced, giving rise to what we could call the "specialty gig economy". This new era heralds a shift towards highly skilled, specialized professionals who seek project-based work that aligns with their expertise and passions. Companies that wish to tap into this premium talent pool must adapt their engagement and management practices. They'll need to offer compelling projects, competitive compensation, and perhaps most crucially, a sense of belonging and purpose to these high-caliber individuals.

Preparing for these changes requires more than just a strategic pivot; it demands a cultural revolution within organizations. The future of contingent workforce management will see companies fostering inclusivity, where the lines between permanent and contingent staff blur. Creating an environment where all talent feels valued and integrated will be key to attracting and retaining the best. Think along the lines of shared learning platforms, team-building activities that include contingent workers, and clear communication channels that keep everyone in the loop.

To wrap it up, the coming years are set to unleash a whirlwind of innovation and transformation in the realm of contingent workforce management. By staying ahead of technological advancements and evolving workforce trends, companies can prepare themselves for the future. Embracing flexibility, fostering a culture of inclusivity, and leveraging technology will be the golden tickets to thriving in this new era. So, let's gear up for an exciting journey into the future, where the possibilities are as limitless as our imagination allows.

Technological Innovations Shaping the Future

Technological innovations are not just playing a role in contingent workforce management; they're leading the charge into the future. As we dive into the myriad of developments that are shaping the horizon, we can't help but marvel at the ways technology is set to revolutionize how we source, manage, and engage contingent labor.

Starting with the big guns, let's talk about Artificial Intelligence (AI) and machine learning. These aren't just buzzwords reserved for tech conferences and sci-fi movies anymore. In the realm of contingent workforce management, AI is transforming the game by enabling smarter, more efficient candidate matching processes. Imagine a system that not only understands the requirements of a job posting but also sifts through vast pools of candidates to identify the perfect match based on skills, experience, and even work style preferences. This is not a distant dream but a rapidly approaching reality.

Next in line, we have blockchain technology. At its core, blockchain offers a level of security, transparency, and efficiency that's unprecedented. For contingent workforce management, this means a future where contracts, payments, and even identity verification are handled with unprecedented ease and trust. The potential here is vast, ranging from simplifying onboarding processes to ensuring compliance and mitigating fraud.

But it's not just AI and blockchain that are stirring the pot. The Internet of Things (IoT) is also stepping into the frame, offering a host of opportunities for enhancing worker productivity and safety. For instance, wearable IoT devices can monitor a worker's environment for safety hazards, offering real-time data to prevent accidents. Moreover, these technologies can track performance and health metrics, ensuring that workers are not only effective but also healthy and safe on the job.

Let's not overlook the role of Virtual and Augmented Reality (VR and AR) in training and development. These tools can simulate real-life work scenarios, offering contingent workers hands-on experience in a controlled, virtual environment. This is particularly beneficial in industries where on-the-job training can be hazardous or impractical.

In the background of these disruptive technologies, we see the relentless march of cloud computing. Cloud-based platforms are making it possible for businesses to manage their contingent workforce from anywhere, at any time, with unprecedented scalability and flexibility. These platforms are becoming more intuitive, offering dashboards and analytics that provide insights into performance, cost, and compliance metrics in real-time.

While we're talking tech, let's not forget about the platforms that are streamlining the entire contingent workforce management process. From sourcing to payment, comprehensive platforms are integrating AI, Big Data, and advanced analytics to offer end-to-end solutions that simplify and enhance every aspect of managing contingent labor.

Speaking of Big Data, it's worth mentioning its critical role in strategic decision-making. By analyzing vast amounts of data on hiring trends, costs, and performance outcomes, organizations can make informed decisions that align with their strategic objectives. The power of predictive analytics, in this context, can't be understated, offering foresights that can significantly optimize contingent workforce strategies.

Moving to a more engaging aspect, gamification is making its mark on contingent workforce management. By incorporating game-design elements in recruitment and training processes, companies can enhance engagement, motivation, and learning outcomes. It's a creative approach that leverages technology to make otherwise mundane tasks exciting and interactive.

Furthermore, the advancement in mobile technology has dramatically impacted how we manage contingent workforces. Mobile apps offer immediate access to job postings, training materials, and communication tools, facilitating a more flexible and responsive workforce. The future here points towards even greater integration, with mobile technology becoming a central hub for managing work-life in the contingent ecosystem.

As we ponder the potential of these technologies, it's clear that ethics and data privacy will play a pivotal role in shaping their adoption. With great power comes great responsibility, and as such, implementing these technological solutions will require a careful balancing act to ensure privacy concerns are adequately addressed and ethical standards are upheld.

Indeed, the future of contingent workforce management is teeming with possibilities. However, it's also accompanied by challenges, not least of which is ensuring that the human element isn't lost amidst the buzz of innovation. Balancing technology with the intrinsic value of human insight and interaction will be key to realizing the full potential of these advances.

The future looks not just bright but downright dazzling with the spectrum of technological innovations on the horizon. As we march towards this future, it's essential for contingent workforce leaders, talent consultants, and companies at large to stay informed and adaptable. The goal isn't just to implement technology for the sake of it but to leverage these innovations in a way that enhances efficiency, engagement, and overall effectiveness of contingent workforce management.

The journey ahead is undoubtedly an exciting one. With each technological breakthrough, we're not just reshaping how we manage contingent labor; we're redefining the possibilities of what contingent workforce can achieve. It's a thrilling time to be at the intersection of contingent workforce management and technological innovation, and the road ahead is ripe with opportunities for those ready to embrace the future.

Preparing for the Evolution of the Contingent Workforce

Gone are the days when employment was a straightforward affair - full-time jobs, benefits, and retirement plans. In today's gig economy, contingent workers, freelancers, and independent contractors are becoming increasingly significant players. Looking at the future, we can see that the contingent workforce is not just a temporary trend but a powerful force changing the environment. For talent consultants, contingent workforce leaders, and organizations that want to navigate this change successfully, it's essential to be ready. So, let's embark on this journey of preparation without tripping over your shoelaces!

First off, understanding the fluid nature of the contingent workforce is crucial. Imagine trying to catch a fish with your bare hands in a bustling stream; that's how dynamic this workforce is. The ability to swiftly adapt to changing demands and trends in the workforce requires a blend of flexibility and foresight. Companies need to cultivate an environment that is not just reactive but proactive, anticipating shifts before they happen.

Technology will play a starring role in this evolution. Just as smartphones turned many of us into amateur photographers, advancements in technology will transform how we manage the contingent workforce. Artificial intelligence, machine learning, and blockchain are not just buzzwords but tools that will drive efficiency and transparency in talent acquisition, management, and payment processes. So, it's time to befriend these technologies and leverage them to your advantage.

Data, the elixir of the digital age, will become increasingly vital. But, collecting data is akin to sipping water from a fire hose if you don't know how to harness its power. The future belongs to those who not only collect but also intelligently analyze data to glean insights on workforce trends, talent needs, and performance metrics. Such data-driven strategies will enable customization and optimization of the contingent workforce program, ensuring that the right talent meets the right opportunity at the right time.

Vendor management will also undergo a transformation. As the contingent workforce grows, managing a slew of vendor relationships will resemble juggling more balls than you have hands. The focus will shift from merely managing these relationships to fostering strategic partnerships. Collaborating with vendors who are not just suppliers but partners in your success story will be key. This requires a keen eye for evaluating vendors beyond their sales pitches and identifying those who genuinely align with your organizational values and goals.

The legal and regulatory environment, always a challenge to deal with, will become even more complicated. As the boundaries between regular and temporary work become less clear, keeping up with compliance requirements will be like deciphering old symbols. But don't worry! Establishing a strong legal foundation and being attentive will protect your organization from possible legal traps, ensuring easy progress.

Speaking of navigation, the role of leadership in steering the contingent workforce strategy cannot be underestimated. As the captains of the ship, leaders must chart a clear course, communicate the vision effectively, and foster a culture that embraces and integrates contingent workers. This means shattering the glass ceilings and erasing the line in the sand between "us" (permanent employees) and "them" (contingent workers), bridging the gap to create a unified, purpose-driven team.

Educating and training your workforce, both contingent and permanent, is another crucial preparation step. As the adage goes, "Give a man a fish, and you feed him for a day. Teach a man to fish, and you feed him for a lifetime." Investing in education and development will not only improve the skill set of your workforce but also drive engagement and loyalty. The future workforce is a learning workforce, hungry for growth and development opportunities.

Understanding the psychological makeup of the contingent worker is also essential. Unlike traditional employees, contingent workers seek flexibility, autonomy, and the opportunity to work on diverse projects. Catering to these needs while ensuring alignment with organizational goals will be a tightrope walk requiring solid emotional intelligence and empathy.

Furthermore, building a culture that supports contingent workers is no longer optional but necessary. A culture that values diversity, inclusion, and flexibility will not only attract top talent but also foster innovation and creativity. Remember, culture eats strategy for breakfast, so make sure your organizational culture is a Michelin-starred banquet that welcomes everyone to the table.

Employee engagement strategies will also need a revamp. With a workforce that's not bound by the traditional 9-to-5 and office walls, engagement must transcend physical boundaries. Creating a sense of belonging and community among contingent workers, who might feel like islands in a vast ocean, will require innovative approaches and communication channels.

Lastly, preparing for the future means embracing uncertainty and building resilience. The only constant in life is change, and the world of contingent work is no exception. Developing a resilient workforce and organization that can bend but not break in the face of adversity will be the ultimate preparation.

In conclusion, preparing for the evolution of the contingent workforce is akin to preparing for a marathon in uncharted territory. It's a journey that requires insight, agility, and a healthy dose of humor to navigate the pitfalls and opportunities that lie ahead. But fear not, brave travelers! With the right preparation, the evolving contingent workforce offers a world of possibilities to explore.

As we stand on the brink of this evolution, it's time to let go of outdated paradigms and embrace the future. The contingent workforce is not just changing the way we work; it's redefining the very fabric of work. So, lace up your shoes, adjust your mindset, and let's embark on this exciting journey together. The future awaits, and it's looking mighty bright from here.

Chapter 12: Building a Culture That Supports the Contingent Workforce

Today's workforce includes more contingent labor than ever before, adding diversity and dynamism to the workforce. But here's the catch - making a work environment that fully supports contingent workers goes beyond offering perks like a pool table or a taco night. It's about creating a culture where every worker, whether they are a full-time employee or a short-term contractor, feels equally respected and engaged. This chapter explores how to build such a culture, one where contingent workers are not just an addition but a core part of the organizational fabric.

First things first, integration is key. Beyond just inclusion in meetings, ensure that contingent workers are provided with clear and open communication channels that keep them engaged and informed. Virtual meetings, project management tools, and regular check-ins can bridge the gap between remote or hybrid contingent workers and full-time staff, making integration a seamless part of the workflow. Instead, it's about ensuring contingent workers have clear goals, understand their role in the larger mission, and, crucially, are given a voice. This could be anything from inviting them to strategic meetings, to offering platforms where their feedback can not only be heard but acted upon. Think of it as making them feel like they're part of the band, not just session musicians brought in to fill the gaps. After all, a sense of belonging can significantly magnify a worker's contribution and commitment to a project.

However, building a supportive culture doesn't end with integration. It also involves creating an inclusive environment where diversity is not just celebrated but seen as a potent catalyst for innovation and growth. This means recognizing the unique perspectives and skills contingent workers bring to the table and ensuring they have equal access to opportunities and resources. By doing so, companies not only stand out as forward-thinking employers but also harness the full potential of their workforce to stay ahead in the game. In the end, supporting contingent workers is not just about ticking a box for HR; it's about weaving a stronger, more vibrant tapestry of talent that can propel an organization to new heights.

Integrating Contingent Workers into Organizational Culture

Let's dive into the intriguing world of contingent workers and their integration into organizational culture. As the contingent workforce continues to burgeon, establishing a culture that embraces diversity, flexibility, and inclusivity isn't just an option; it's imperative.

The core challenge here isn't about merely adding contingent workers to the mix. It's about reimagining what inclusivity looks like in a dynamic, ever-evolving workforce. This journey begins with understanding the unique value each contingent worker brings to the table - their skills, their flexibility, and their fresh perspectives.

First off, let's tackle communication. It's the golden thread that ties everything together. Effective communication strategies ensure that contingent workers are not only aware of organizational goals but feel a part of their achievement. This includes everything from onboarding processes to regular updates, making sure everyone's on the same page, no matter their contract duration or location.

Another key aspect is recognition. Just because someone isn't on the payroll full-time doesn't mean their contributions are any less significant. Regardless of contract length or employment type, contributions from contingent workers should be recognized at the same level as full-time staff. Establishing recognition programs tailored to contingent workers, such as achievement awards or feedback platforms, reinforces their value and motivates high performance. Recognizing the achievements of contingent workers reinforces their value to the organization, motivates them, and fosters a sense of belonging.

Training plays a pivotal role too. Investing in the development of contingent workers not only enhances their performance but also demonstrates the organization's commitment to their professional growth. This could range from in-house training sessions to access to external courses and workshops.

Then there's the challenge of building connections. Traditional team-building activities might not always fit the bill, considering the diverse schedules and locations of contingent workers. Virtual team-building exercises, flexible scheduling of events, and social platforms can help bridge this gap, facilitating interaction and camaraderie.

Leadership involvement is crucial. Leaders set the tone for organizational culture. Their active participation in integrating contingent workers—be it through direct interaction, inclusion in decision-making, or public acknowledgment of their work— sends a powerful message about their value to the organization.

Feedback mechanisms shouldn't be overlooked. Just because contingent workers might not be around as long, doesn't mean their insights and experiences aren't valuable. Regular, structured feedback sessions help in addressing any issues and leveraging opportunities for improvement.

Creating a sense of community among all workers, irrespective of their employment status, is essential. This could be achieved through shared online platforms, social events, and common spaces, fostering an environment of mutual respect and understanding.

It's also about leveling the playing field. Ensuring contingent workers have access to the same resources, from technology to workspace amenities, as permanent employees do, negates an 'us vs. them' mentality and promotes inclusivity.

Policies and practices need to reflect the values of inclusivity and diversity. This means going beyond mere compliance with legal requirements to crafting policies that actively support the integration of contingent workers into the organizational fabric.

Innovation in integration techniques is key. From gamification of onboarding processes to personalized career paths, the goal is to continually seek out new ways to enhance the contingent worker experience.

Adaptability cannot be overstated. As the external environment and organizational needs evolve, so too must the strategies for integrating contingent workers. This agility not only benefits the workers but strengthens the organization's resilience and competitive edge.

Finally, it's about celebrating diversity. Contingent workers often bring different backgrounds, experiences, and perspectives. Recognizing and leveraging this diversity can drive innovation, enhance problem-solving, and lead to more informed decision-making.

Integrating contingent workers into organizational culture is more than a set of strategies. It's a mindset that views every worker as an integral part of the organization's ecosystem, contributing to its vibrancy, flexibility, and growth. It's about building a culture where every worker, whether they are a full-time employee or a short-term contractor, feels equally respected and engaged. Success in achieving this culture can be measured by monitoring retention rates, engagement levels through surveys, and performance indicators specific to contingent workers. Metrics such as time-to-productivity, satisfaction scores, and their rate of involvement in innovation initiatives are key to gauging their integration and engagement.

As we move forward, remember that the goal isn't to blur the distinctions between contingent and permanent workers but to value each individual's contribution, ensuring everyone feels valued, supported, and part of something bigger than themselves. This, my friends, is the secret sauce to not just surviving but thriving in the dynamic world of work.

Creating an Inclusive Environment for All Workers

Before we move on from the topic of integrating contingent workers into organizational culture, let's highlight the importance of building an inclusive environment that embraces all workers. This goes beyond meeting the standards for diversity and inclusion; it's about creating a culture where every person, whether full-time or contingent, feels respected and motivated. Let's explore some approaches that make your workspace not only inclusive but also stimulating.

Inclusion starts at the top. Leadership must not only preach inclusivity but also practice it in visible, tangible ways. This means recognizing contingent workers in company meetings, involving them in relevant decision-making processes, and ensuring their contributions are acknowledged and celebrated. It's not just about making them feel included; it's about showing everyone that these practices are the norm, not the exception.

Clear communication channels are the backbone of an inclusive environment. But here's the twist: it's not just about ensuring messages get from point A to B. It's about open, two-way streets where feedback and ideas flow freely in both directions. By empowering contingent workers to voice their opinions and suggestions without fear of reprisal, you create a culture of mutual respect and collaboration.

Training programs are often seen as the bread and butter of employee development. However, these programs often inadvertently exclude contingent workers. By designing training initiatives that are accessible to all staff, including contingent workers, you foster a learning culture that benefits everyone. After all, today's contingent worker could be tomorrow's full-time superstar.

Now, let's talk about workspace design. It might seem trivial, but the physical workspace can significantly impact inclusivity. Co-locating contingent workers with full-time staff, providing access to the same resources, and ensuring they have a space to call their own can make a world of difference. It's about erasing the lines of division and promoting unity.

But what about the remote workforce? In today's digital age, inclusivity extends beyond physical walls to virtual workspaces. Ensuring that remote meetings are accessible, promoting regular check-ins, and providing virtual networking opportunities are just as crucial for inclusion. In essence, digital inclusivity must mirror physical efforts, ensuring no one is left behind.

Recognition is another key element. Everyone wants to feel appreciated, and contingent workers are no exception. Creating an awards system that also acknowledges the achievements and contributions of contingent staff can significantly enhance their sense of belonging and value within the company.

Another effective strategy is to establish inclusive committees or task forces that include contingent workers. These groups can focus on various aspects of workplace diversity and inclusion, providing a platform for all voices to be heard and contributing to a more inclusive environment.

The integration of contingent workers into social and networking events is also paramount. These interactions shouldn't just be about work. Social events, team-building activities, and informal gatherings can bridge gaps, build relationships, and dismantle any 'us vs. them' mentality that might have crept into the workplace.

Creating inclusive policies that explicitly mention contingent workers is another critical step. This might include adjustments to existing policies or the development of new ones that address the unique needs and circumstances of contingent workers. Ensuring these policies are clearly communicated and easily accessible is equally important.

Mentorship programs can be a powerful tool for inclusion. Pairing contingent workers with experienced colleagues can help them navigate the workplace, build professional networks, and develop career paths. It's about providing support and guidance that extends beyond the confines of their contract.

Feedback mechanisms specifically designed for contingent workers can offer insights into their workplace experience. This feedback is invaluable for identifying areas of improvement and developing strategies to enhance inclusivity. It's a proactive approach to ensuring all workers feel valued and heard.

One must not overlook the role of technology in creating an inclusive environment. Utilizing collaborative tools and platforms that facilitate easy communication and access to information helps in bridging the gap between different categories of workers. It's about leveraging technology to create a unified workforce.

Lastly, celebrating cultural diversity within the workforce, including contingent workers, enriches the workplace experience for everyone. Cultural events, awareness programs, and diversity training can promote understanding and appreciation of different perspectives, contributing to a genuinely inclusive environment.

Creating an inclusive environment for all workers, including those on contingent contracts, requires a multifaceted approach. It's about leadership commitment, clear communication, accessibility, recognition, policy inclusivity, mentorship, feedback, leveraging technology, and celebrating diversity. By implementing these strategies, companies can ensure that their workforce not only thrives but also fosters a culture of inclusivity and respect that attracts top talent in today's competitive market.

Wrap-Up Round Up

As we reach the culmination of our exploration into the contingent workforce industry, it's essential to recognize the transformative journey we've embarked upon together. Navigating through the intricate maze of contingent labor, from the foundational understanding to the complex dynamics of program governance, vendor management, and future trends, has been nothing short of a thrilling adventure. It's been a narrative woven with the threads of strategy, compliance, and innovation, tailored to fit the unique fabric of contingent workforce leadership and consulting.

The chapters have methodically peeled back the layers of the contingent workforce ecosystem, revealing its multifaceted character. We've traversed from the basics of understanding this industry's very foundation to grappling with the nuances of vendor neutrality and the pivotal role of technology in reshaping the industry of talent management. At each turn, the goal remained steadfast—to furnish you, the talent consultants, program consultants, and contingent workforce leaders, with a comprehensive toolkit to navigate this domain adeptly.

Embarking on this journey, we acknowledged the challenge of distilling a subject as dynamic as the contingent workforce into tangible insights. Yet, through a blend of persuasive narrative, delightful humor, and clear expository, we've aimed to make each concept accessible and relatable. The essence of contingency labor's appeal—its fluidity, diversity, and adaptability—has been mirrored in our approach to unraveling its complexities.

The immersion into vendor management systems (VMS), the differentiation between Managed Service Provider (MSP) and

Internal Project Management Office (PMO), and the exploration of artificial intelligence (AI) in talent management have not just been academic exercises. These sections aimed to ignite a spark of curiosity, encouraging a deeper dive into how technology and strategic thinking can revolutionize the way organizations engage with contingent labor.

In addressing classifications of contractors, the legal and regulatory considerations, and the art of building a culture that embraces contingent workers, we've not shied away from the tough conversations. These discussions were pivotal, setting the stage for a holistic understanding of the contingent workforce ecosystem. They serve as reminders of the importance of embracing diversity, ensuring compliance, and fostering an inclusive environment for all workers.

The narrative has consistently shown that the contingent workforce is more than a business strategy—it's a dynamic, growing community. It's a result of the changing work environment, motivated by people who want flexibility, diversity, and independence. Acknowledging this human aspect is essential—it's what makes policies, programs, and practices alive, transforming them from ideas into the core of organizations.

The conversations on supplier management strategies, the engagement process, and the anticipatory gaze toward future trends were all directed towards one end—empowering you to make informed, strategic decisions that not only benefit the organization but also support the contingent workers who contribute to its success. These sections highlighted the importance of viewing contingent workforce management not as a static function but as a dynamic, integral part of the broader talent management strategy.

Incorporating AI into the contingent workforce narrative wasn't just about showcasing technological advancements. It was a nod to the necessity of staying ahead of the curve, leveraging technology to enhance decision-making, efficiency, and ultimately, competitiveness. Just as AI evolves, so too must our strategies for engaging, managing, and integrating contingent labor within our organizational ecosystems.

The expectation of upcoming changes highlighted an essential message: the work environment is constantly changing. Being passive is not an option. Getting ready for the development of the flexible workforce demands flexibility, vision, and a strong dedication to innovation. It challenges us to think creatively, to picture a future where the use of temporary labor is smooth, deliberate, and mutually beneficial.

As we conclude, it's pertinent to circle back to our starting point—the imperative of understanding. Knowledge, as we've seen, is the cornerstone of effective contingent workforce management. But beyond knowledge, it's the application, the thoughtful integration of insights into practice, that propels us forward. This book aimed to bridge that gap, offering a guidepost for navigating the complexities of contingent workforce management with confidence, creativity, and a dash of humor.

The role of talent consultants, program consultants, and contingent workforce leaders is more critical now than ever. In your hands lies the power to shape the future of work, to lead with vision, empathy, and strategic acumen. The path forward is one of partnership—between organizations, contingent workers, and the communities that support them. It's a journey of continuous learning, adaptation, and innovation.

As you move forward, armed with the insights and strategies discussed, remember that the story of the contingent workforce is still being written. You are not just observers but active participants, authors of the next chapters. Your actions, decisions, and leadership will define the future contours of contingent labor, making it more inclusive, strategic, and impactful.

In closing, let this book not be a final word but a launching pad for deeper exploration, conversation, and action. The contingent workforce industry awaits, ripe with challenges to overcome and opportunities to seize. Here's to navigating this journey with insight, integrity, and a touch of humor. Here's to shaping the future of work, together.

Appendix A: Appendix

So, you've made it all the way through to the appendix, huh? Well, pat yourself on the back because the journey through the contingent workforce industry is no small feat. But let's not rest on our laurels ... at least, not just yet. The world of contingent labor is ever evolving, and it's essential to stay on top of the game. That's right, the quest for knowledge never ends, and for that very reason, we've packed this section with additional resources to ensure you're always in the know.

Resources for Contingent Workforce Management

Imagine having a toolbox. Inside this toolbox, you've got everything you need to fix a leaky tap, assemble furniture, or even build a house. This appendix? It's kind of like your toolbox for navigating the contingent workforce landscape.

But enough with the analogies—let's dive into the meat of the matter:

1. **Professional Associations:** Joining organizations like the Staffing Industry Analysts (SIA) or the American Staffing Association (ASA) can be invaluable. These groups provide a treasure trove of research, networking opportunities, and industry insights that are just waiting to be explored.

2. **Online Forums and Discussion Groups:** Sites like LinkedIn and Reddit host vibrant communities of contingent workforce professionals. Here, you can ask questions, share experiences, and gain access to a wealth of informal knowledge that's both current and practical.

3. **Vendor Management System (VMS) Providers:**
VMS solutions are crucial for effectively managing a contingent workforce. Familiarize yourself with top providers by attending webinars, demos, and reading case studies to understand how their solutions can streamline your contingent labor program.

4. **Regulatory Updates:** Keeping abreast of labor laws and regulations is non-negotiable. Resources such as the Department of Labor's website or legal blogs specializing in employment law can be excellent sources of up-to-date information.

5. **Continuous Learning Platforms:** Investing in your education or that of your team's is invaluable. Platforms like Coursera, Udemy, or LinkedIn Learning offer courses on everything from human resources management to data analytics, all of which can enhance your contingent workforce program.

Case Study / Whitepaper Bibliography

1. Advantage xPO: "Contingent Workforce Optimization – A Global Medical Device Manufacturing Company" (2024). Available at this link: https://www.advantagexpo-us.com/global-assets/assets/doc/xPO-CW-Medical_Equipment_Production-REV100720.pdf
2. Aerotek: "Maximizing Your Contingent Workforce." Available at this link: https://www.aerotek.com/-/media/files/aerotek/pdfs/thought-leadership/cacq1_aerotek_maximizing_contingent_workforce_white_paper.pdf
3. Ingenovis Health: "Strategies for Effective Contingent Nurse Workforce Management" (2024). Available at this link: https://www.aha.org/system/files/media/file/2024/02/Ingenovis_NurseWorforceMgmt_KE_022724.pdf
4. Nelson, A.: "Contingent worker engagement best practices" (2014, October 1). Staffing Industry Analysts Advisory Group (SIAAG).
5. Pontoon Solutions: "Considerations for interagency guidance on third party risk management" (June 2023). Available at this link: https://www.pontoonsolutions.com/en/insights/all/pontoons-perspective-considerations-for-interagency-guidance-on-third-party-risk-management-tprm/
6. Pontoon Solutions: Talent leaders guide: Finding the right MSP partner (No publication year given). Available at this link: https://www.pontoonsolutions.com/en/insights/all/talent-leaders-guide-finding-the-right-msp-partner/

7. Retkowsky, Jana, et al.: "Toward a sustainable career perspective on contingent work: A critical review and a research agenda" (2023). *Career Development International*, 28(1), 1-18. DOI: 10.1108/CDI-06-2022-0181.

8. Accenture: "Setting Up for Skilling Up: Henkel's Smart Bet for Innovation and Growth from Sustained Upskilling Efforts" (2021). Available at this link: https://www.nationalacademyhr.org/sites/default/fil es/2021%20CHRO%20Academy%20/Additional%20 Content/Accenture-Henkel-CaseStudy-Long-Narrative.pdf

9. World Economic Forum, Accenture, SkyHive, & Unilever: "Future Skills Pilot Report: Thinking Outside the Box to Reimagine Talent Mobility" (2021).

Additional Resources for Contingent Workforce Management

The contingent workforce industry can be very complex and challenging to navigate, as if you were trying to do a difficult puzzle without seeing, while balancing on one wheel. But don't worry! This appendix is meant to be your helpful guide in the huge universe of resources for contingent workforce management.

Let's start with industry associations and thought leadership organizations. These groups, such as the Staffing Industry Analysts (SIA) and the American Staffing Association (ASA), are very valuable sources of information, and not only for their white papers (which are like industry guides). Their conferences are like the ultimate staffing events — without the dirt and bad decisions — providing great networking opportunities, current topics, and insights that are unique.

Then we have the ever-useful Vendor Management Systems (VMS). Remember that VMS is not just a tool; it's your best friend in managing contingent labor. It keeps track of your contingent workforce, so you don't have to. Think of it as the Alfred to your Batman in your contingent workforce program. Selecting the right VMS involves understanding its functions and features, yes, but also recognizing its ability to gel with your organization's unique culture and needs.

Now, for those looking to deep dive into best practices and case studies, academic journals might not be the first resource that springs to mind. But, oh, they should be. Journals such as the Journal of Business Logistics or the Harvard Business Review offer cutting-edge research and analysis. It's like having access to a contingent workforce sage who can provide you with the wisdom of the ages (or at least the latest and greatest in industry innovation).

Let's not overlook the power of technology and AI. In an age where Siri can remind you to call your mom, AI can also revolutionize how you manage your contingent workforce. Tools leveraging AI for talent acquisition and management can turn the Herculean task of managing a diversified workforce into a walk in the park. There are numerous platforms and applications dedicated to this very purpose, blending the latest in tech to offer solutions that are not just efficient but also scalable.

Consulting firms and specialized contingent workforce advisors also offer a treasure trove of expertise. Whether it's navigating legal landscapes or designing an effective program structure, these wizards of the workforce can offer tailored advice that fits your organizational needs like a glove. Think of them as the personal trainers of the contingent workforce world — getting your program into shape, no sweat!

But hey, why stop there? Webinars and online courses offer flexible, on-the-go learning opportunities for those whose schedules look like a Tetris game on level expert. Platforms like Coursera, LinkedIn Learning, and Udemy host courses that range from the basics of contingent workforce management to advanced strategic planning and analytics.

And speaking of analytics, let's talk data. In the world of contingent workforce management, data is king, queen, and the royal court. Utilizing workforce analytics tools can give you insights into your program that you might not have realized you needed, helping to optimize your workforce strategy and justify future investments.

Peer networking groups, both online and in real life, are also invaluable. There's nothing quite like learning from those who have walked the path before you. These groups offer a platform for sharing experiences, challenges, and successes. Sometimes, it's just comforting to know that someone else out there understands the unique challenges of trying to explain what you do at a family dinner.

For those with an eye on the future, keeping abreast of technological innovations shaping contingent workforce management is crucial. There are several foresight and innovation hubs, as well as tech-focused conferences, that can keep you on the cutting edge, ensuring that your strategies are not only responsive to current trends but are also forward-thinking.

Creating a culture that supports the contingent workforce is another aspect where resources abound, from books and podcasts to webinars focusing on diversity, equity, inclusion, and belonging. These resources can help integrate contingent workers into your organizational fabric, weaving a tapestry of inclusivity that enhances both morale and productivity.

Government and regulatory resources also play a critical role, keeping you tethered to the ground with the necessary compliance and legal frameworks. Websites of labor departments or equivalent bodies in your country are instrumental in ensuring that your contingent workforce program doesn't inadvertently step into murky legal waters.

Supplier management is yet another critical area where armfuls of resources can be drafted to your aid. From supplier performance evaluation tools to relationship management strategies, the right resources can ensure that your suppliers are not just vendors but are true partners in your contingent workforce mission.

Finally, one cannot underestimate the power of books. Yes, good old-fashioned print on paper (or e-books if you prefer). There are numerous publications out there dedicated to contingent workforce management, offering insights, strategies, and advice that cover the gamut from beginner basics to expert esoterica.

It's clear that whether you're a seasoned contingent workforce leader or a company just dipping your toes into the contingent labor pool, there's a vast ocean of resources at your disposal. The trick is not just in finding these resources but also in leveraging them effectively to craft a contingent workforce program that's as strategic as it is compliant, as efficient as it is humane. May the force of the contingent workforce be with you!

Glossary of Terms

In the realm of contingent workforce management, wandering into the jargon jungle without a guide can leave even the most seasoned professionals scratching their heads. But worry not! We have assembled a snappy glossary to help demystify this specialized lingo, making the path clearer and maybe, just a smidge more entertaining. Let's dive into the terms that pepper our discussions about contingent labor, without stepping into the deep end of already-covered territories in other chapters.

Contingent Workforce

A labor pool consisting of folks who are not on the permanent payroll but are on deck for projects or specific periods. It's what you get when you mix flexibility, a dash of freedom, and the modern work ethos. Think freelancers, independent contractors, consultants, and sometimes, that guy you call when the proverbial office printer catches fire (figuratively, I hope).

Managed Service Provider (MSP)

A majestic conductor waving their baton over the chaos of contingent workforce management, ensuring harmony and efficiency. An MSP takes the heavy lifting off your shoulders, managing suppliers, processes, and technologies. Sort of like having your very own labor orchestra maestro.

Vendor Management System (VMS)

This tech marvel is the backstage crew to the MSP's conductor, a software platform that does everything from manage job requests to handle financials and reporting. It's the unsung hero that makes sure the contingent work symphony plays on without a hitch.

Independent Contractor

A different kind of worker, but someone who manages their own work. They provide their services on a contract basis, independent from the usual ties of employment. Like a career ninja, they join your organization, produce high-quality work, and disappear without a trace—onto the next challenge.

Vendor Neutrality

A principle ensuring that when you choose a contingent workforce solution, you're getting an unbiased selection of talent suppliers. It's like a talent buffet, where every dish gets a fair chance to be sampled, ensuring no single supplier hogs the limelight (or the budget).

Program Management Office (PMO)

Your strategic sidekick in navigating the contingent workforce industry. Unlike MSP, the PMO is typically an internal (company self-run) team dedicated to governance, standards, and achieving business goals. Think of it as the homegrown hero of contingent workforce strategy for the company.

Classification Compliance

The delicate balance of classifying workers correctly to prevent legal mistakes and financial disasters. It's making sure that your temporary workforce doesn't unintentionally become employees, setting off a cascade of regulatory obligations and possible legal troubles.

Artificial Intelligence (AI)

The intelligent helper that's transforming the way we search, recruit, and oversee temporary workers. From matching algorithms to chatbots that support the confused candidate, AI is the clever tool that's making the future of work fascinating (and a bit futuristic).

And that's it, the best of the best of contingent workforce terms that you might encounter. Whether you're planning over coffee or navigating the complexity of compliance, this glossary will be the reliable guide you didn't know you needed. Now, go ahead and use the language of contingent workforce expertise with assurance (and a touch of flair).

Legal and Compliance Checklist for Contingent Workforce Programs

You've managed the tricky aspects of contingent workforce management and reached the important stage of Legal and Compliance. You might be tempted to relax now, but don't be too hasty. Developing a strong contingent workforce program is not only about planning; it's also avoiding any potential legal troubles. So, let's go over the basics with some humor and insight to keep things interesting.

One of the first things you need to do is figure out the legal situation, which is like reading an old map. The laws and rules can vary from one place to another, so you need to understand the local, state, and federal laws that apply to temporary workers. This is not only about knowing the past legal developments; it's also about expecting future changes in the legal situation.

Here's a hint: if you think you're covered by a one-size-fits-all approach, you're probably about to walk the plank. Differentiating between independent contractors and employees is a nuanced affair, fraught with complexities and potential misclassification pitfalls. This is not just about the classification itself, but also involves understanding the correct tax forms and implications, benefits, and insurance requirements.

Speaking of insurance, let's not forget the potential storms brewing around worker's compensation and liability insurance. Ensuring your contingent workers are adequately covered isn't just a nice-to-have; it's a must-have to avoid legal thunderstorms. It's time to ask yourself, "Do my contingent workforce programs have the necessary insurance umbrellas open?"

Next, pay close attention to the contractual agreements with your staffing providers or Managed Service Providers (MSPs). These documents are the keel that keeps your contingent workforce ship stable in turbulent waters. They should clearly define the roles, responsibilities, and expectations of all parties involved, ensuring compliance is maintained throughout the engagement.

Lastly, we can't forget about data protection and privacy laws. In an age where information is more precious than buried treasure, ensuring the confidentiality and security of your contingent workers' data is paramount. Failure to comply with regulations like GDPR or CCPA doesn't just risk a slap on the wrist; it risks capsizing your entire program.

To summarize, navigating the legal and compliance aspects of contingent workforce management is a bit like being a skilled sailor; you need to be vigilant, adaptable, and prepared for what lies on the horizon. Keeping abreast of legal changes, understanding the fine print of contracts, properly classifying your workforce, and ensuring all legal and insurance requirements are met are your compass points. Stay true to these, and your journey through the contingent workforce waters will be both prosperous and compliant.

Remember, this checklist isn't just a formality; it's your map to avoiding the sirens' call of legal peril. Use it wisely, and you'll navigate your contingent workforce program to the treasure chest of success and compliance.